Selected Plays
of
Alphonse Allais

Other Books by Doug Skinner

The Unknown Adjective and Other Stories

—translations—

Three Dreams
by G. B. Nazari

Considerations on the Death and Burial of Tristan Tzara
by Isidore Isou

How I Became an Idiot by Francisque Sarcey
by Alphonse Allais

Captain Cap: His Adventures, His Ideas, His Drinks
by Alphonse Allais

Merde à La Belle Époque: Scatological Texts
by Various

Selected Plays

of

Alphonse Allais

COMPILED & TRANSLATED FROM THE FRENCH BY
DOUG SKINNER

**BLACK
SCAT
BOOKS**

2014

Selected Plays of Alphonse Allais

Compiled & Translated from the French by Doug Skinner

ISBN 978-0692275085

First Edition

Cover and book design: Norman Conquest

Illustrations on the frontis and facing page
are by Doug Skinner.

Black Scat Books
Publishers of Sublime Art & Literature
BlackScatBooks.com

Table of Contents

Alphonse Allais Saunters Before the Footlights

Alphonse Allais, the son of a pharmacist in Honfleur, went to Paris in 1872 to learn the family trade. Much to his parents' dismay, he showed far more interest in the artistic ferment and Bohemian freedom of Montmartre. Rather than attend classes, he partied with literary groups like the Hydropathes, Zutistes and Barbus, dated dancers (including Jane Avril, memorably depicted by Toulouse-Lautrec), and drank his fill of the lovely green "parrot," absinthe.

He became a fixture at Le Chat Noir, the cabaret founded by Rodolphe Salis in 1881, famous for its roster of poets and singers and for its shadow puppet plays. Salis ran the place in his own distinctive style, greeting patrons with such pleasantries as "What happened to that other woman?" and "When did you get out of jail?", and refusing to pay performers. Allais edited the weekly paper, filling it with his short stories and commentary, and even played drum for the puppet plays. He also established himself as a formidable "fumiste," a hoaxer and joker. Colleagues and clients were treated to a relentless program of deadpan puns and mystifications. Allais was handsome, blond, and reserved—he was often described as seeming "English"—and his whilom training as a pharmacist set him apart from the usual run of painters and poets.

He also became somewhat of a dramatic critic. Paris's most influential critic, Francisque Sarcey, was an overweight boor who routinely championed common sense, cliche, and lightweight traditional theater. Rather than contest him, Allais simply wrote a column for *Le Chat Noir* under his name. The fictional Francisque became a prattling, lecherous glutton, pompously holding forth on the obvious, complaining about his impotence and constipation, and fulminating against the real Sarcey, whom he claimed was ruining his reputation by writing such stupid stuff for *Le Temps*. Sarcey was a surprisingly good sport about all of this, probably realizing that any protest on his part would make him look even more ridiculous, and that he was outmatched by Allais. It should be added that the Allais Sarcey was also more likely to give rave reviews to productions at Le Chat Noir, and to plug books and plays by its regulars.

Allais later became best known as a humorist and journalist, but his career began in cabaret, and theater was never far from his mind.

One of Allais's closest friends and colleagues, the unique poet-inventor-humorist Charles Cros, created a particularly Montmartrian genre in the 1880s. He wrote a nonsensical little monologue called *Le hareng saur,* which greatly amused the clientele of Le Chat Noir. Allais himself translated it into English in 1880:

THE SONG OF THE "SALT HERRING"

He came along holding in his hands dirty, dirty, dirty,
A big nail pointed, pointed, pointed,
And a hammer heavy, heavy, heavy,
He propped the ladder high, high, high,
Placed the nail pointed, pointed, pointed,
Against the wall—toc! toc! toc!
He tied to the nail a string long, long, long,

And at the end of it a salt herring dry, dry, dry,
Then letting fall the hammer heavy, heavy, heavy,
He got down from the ladder high, high, high,
Picked up the ladder and went away, away, away.
Since then at the end of the string long, long, long,
A salt herring dry, dry, dry,
Has swung slowly, slowly, slowly.
Now I have composed this story simple, simple, simple,
To make all serious men mad, mad, mad,
And to amuse little children tiny, tiny, tiny.

This charming trifle intrigued a young actor known as Coquelin Cadet. His given name was Ernest Alexandre Honoré Coquelin; he was known as "cadet," the younger, to distinguish himself from his older brother, Benoît-Constant, who, among other things, originated the role of Cyrano de Bergerac. Cadet saw that the short comic monologue was an effective vehicle for a young comic actor, and a good way to entertain a cabaret audience. He performed *The Salt Herring* to general approval, and soon added other Cros monologues to his repertory. They became quite popular, sparking such spinoffs as his book *The Art of the Monologue*, and offerings from other writers in his circle. Georges Feydeau even wrote him a monologue called *The Man Who Doesn't Like Monologues.*

Allais contributed a number of them as well. They debuted in *Le Chat Noir*, were performed by Cadet, and were then sometimes released as chapbooks by the publisher Ollendorff.

Allais wrote only one full-fledged play unassisted, a one-act play based on one of his Cadet monologues, *The Miserable Wretch and the Good Genie.* His other efforts were all collaborations. Included here are two that are particularly Allaisian. The first, *Silvérie, or the Dutch Fund,* was based on one of his short stories, and written with Tristan

Bernard. Contemporary evidence suggests that Bernard had more to do with its dramatization than Allais, but the combination was a happy one. The other, *The Polisher*, was written with Albert René, the usual pen name of Albert-René Morice.

Allais contributed to several ephemeral revues, whose surviving scripts mostly attest to the public's fondness for topical song parodies. He probably only lent his name to most of them, which include *Au Moulin de la Galette* (1889), *Revue Libre* (1890), *A la gare comme à la gare* (1899), *Eh! Placide! Eh! Généreux* (1901), and *Chat-Mauve Revue* (1904). He put more work into the three-act comedy *Innocent*, written with Alfred Capus in 1896, about a small town poacher wrongly convicted of assaulting a policeman, and the ensuing political and social complications. It was superseded, however, by the novel that Allais adapted from it, *L'Affaire Blaireau*, which is unalloyed Allais, and improves greatly on the original. Another three-act, *Monsieur La Pudeur (Mister Prude)*, written in 1903 with Félix Galipeau and Paul Bonhomme, is a fairly generic farce about a prude who discovers the pleasures of adultery. Two other one-acts are worth mentioning, both based on previously published stories: *Congé Amiable (Friendly Departure,* 1903), with Tristan Bernard, concerning a couple who break their lease by a subterfuge; and *Aux Consignés! (Assembly!,* 1904), with Henri Darsoy, army hijinks about a canteen owner who is cuckolded by an officer and a wealthy soldier. These last three came in the last few years of Allais's life (he died in 1905), when he was ill, saddled with debt, trapped in a failed marriage, and not at his most inventive; he may have simply sold his name, or the right to use the earlier stories.

In addition to the monologues written for Coquelin Cadet, and the three one-acts mentioned above, I've included a number of skits, dialogues, and burlesques from Allais's columns for *Le Chat Noir*, *Le Journal*, and *Le Sourire*. These show Allais at his most characteristic, and include political satire, he-she sketches, children's stories, a play for dogs, a miniature operetta in rhyme, and the unending skirmishes between writers and their publishers, directors, and censors.

I've prefaced this selection with a piece about Coquelin Cadet, written by Allais as Sarcey. It's just a plug for a joke book by Cadet, but contains a charming verbal portrait of him, and provides a taste of Allais's faux-Francisque. The other pieces are given in chronological order; there are notes in the back. I've kept topical allusions intact, and left Parisian place names in Parisian, to keep the flavor of La Belle Époque; actors who perform the pieces are welcome to substitute references that don't need footnotes.

Doug Skinner
New York City
July, 2014

Coquelin Cadet

Coquelin Cadet

The first time that I saw Coquelin Cadet, I was in a pastry shop across from the Conservatory. I was seated on the mezzanine with a certain Céline (say, that rhymes!), a charming young person whose stomach issued, at frequent intervals, imperious demands for brioche, washed down with countless glasses of Malaga.

Whatever happened to her? If she had wanted to work... but, you know, she was one of those girls whose head was filled with nothing but fun—amusement, she called it.

I wore myself out, repeating, "My little Céline..."

But why, I wonder, am I boring you with this Céline, whom you wouldn't know from Adam and Eve, and whom I myself have relegated to the attic of my oldest memories.

Coquelin Cadet, in that era, was not as old as he is now.

And me, I was younger as well.

It's funny, all the same, this business of time. The more years that go by, the older you get, and after that you die, and then where do you go? Science, which walks with the stride of a giant, has not yet elucidated this cruel enigma, as Bourget calls it.

I liked Coquelin Cadet immediately.

He left the Conservatory with his nose in the air, merry, smiling, fresh, and as pretty as a little pig who has just had a bath.

I said to myself, "There's a lad who will go far."

Someone said, "That's Coquelin's brother."

"Ah," I said, and shook his hand.

Since then, circumstances have shown that I was not mistaken.

Coquelin Cadet has lived up to his promise, and then some.

A charming youth, talented, a musician to his fingertips, adored by the fair sex: there's one creature who must not be bored with life.

Everyone worthy of the name applauds him. Everyone reads him.

Publishers crowd his antechamber.

Paul Ollendorff has purchased entire villas from publications signed by this young member of the Comédie-Française.

His latest, *Pirouettes*, published by our friend Jules Lévy, is in everybody's hands. And let me tell you; you'd have to pull it from them!

As is only just.

You cannot imagine the constant stream of belly laughs that bubbles throughout the pages of this collection.

I quote at random:

In a courtroom:

THE JUDGE: You have beaten your unfortunate wife with a stick.

THE ACCUSED: The doctor prescribed a *vigorous massage*.

General Boulanger to Charles Chincholle:

"What did the sock say when its toe wore out?"

"I haven't the slightest idea."

"Well, it said... darn."

In a salon:

"Do you know that young poet?"

"Yes, he's full of talent; unfortunately, he lets women support him."

"That's too bad, for he's certainly gifted."

"Oh, like Alphonse,[1] he gets plenty of gifts."

A winter thought: in December, it's easy to be cold-blooded.

But I won't insist: you know Coquelin Cadet as well as I.

Only yesterday, I heard him recite the "Rendezvous" by my friend Léon Gandillot. You know, the author of that famous *Clinging Vines* that I was the first to proclaim a great success. Well, Cadet was charming; and it was a triumph for both author and interpreter.

Bravo, Cadet!

FRANCISQUE SARCEY

1. There's no question here of Mr. Alphonse Allais, although that young man's delicacy toward women certainly leaves much to be desired.

A Poor Man

A heartbreaking story sobbed by Coquelin Cadet
for Coquelin Cadet

The man was hungry... and had three sous.

Very hungry... and only three sous!

To his right, a bakery which gives off the intoxicating aroma of freshly baked bread.

And the man doesn't enter... Why?

Because, in addition to his unbelievable appetite, he has within him another... passion, no less imperious, although completely opposed in spirit.

To his left, a small establishment, less genteel than the bakery, yet, on certain occasions, quite useful.

The man hesitates for a while.

Finally, the second... passion overwhelms him, and he turns anxiously to the left.

He enters, gives his three sous to a woman who is very ugly, but extremely dirty, and who indicates an available... cabin, into which he disappears, and there...

There... Oh! How horrible!

Vain attempts!

Nothing! Nothing!! Nothing!!!

The man leaves the cabin, walks through the establishment run by the woman who is very dirty, but extremely ugly, and once again passes the bakery which gives off the intoxicating aroma of freshly baked bread.

My Pal Mittick

One day when it was raining, raining, raining, my pal Mittick was very tired, very tired, very tired, so he crossed a little desert.

And at the end of the desert, my pal Mittick came to a little palm tree, that was as green, green, green, as anything.

And at the foot of the little green palm tree, a little purse that was empty, empty, empty.

Since it was still raining, raining, raining, and since my pal Mittick was still very tired, very tired, very tired, he crossed another little desert, and at the end of the other little desert, my pal Mittick came to another little green palm tree, and at the foot of the other palm tree, a little coin that was all rusty, all rusty, all rusty.

Since it was still raining, my pal Mittick took the little coin that was all rusty, and put it in the little purse, which was then not empty at all...

...That's all...

The Calf

A Christmas story for Sara Salis

— Once upon a time, there was a little boy who was very good, very good. So for Christmas, his papa got him a calf.

— A real one?

— Yes, Sara, a real one.

— With flesh and skin?

— Yes, Sara, with flesh and skin.

— Who walked on his feet?

— I told you, a real calf!

— Then what?

— Then, the little boy was quite pleased to have a little calf. However, because he did dirty things on the living room floor...

— The little boy?

— No, the calf... Because he did dirty things, and made noise, and broke his little sisters' toys...

— The calf had little sisters?

— No, the little boy's little sisters... So he built a shed in the garden, a pretty little wooden shed...

— With little windows?

— Yes, Sara, with lots of little windows, and glass of many colors... That night, it was New Year's Eve. The little boy's papa and mama were invited to a lady's house for dinner. So, after the little boy had his supper, he went to bed and his parents left...

— They left him all alone in the house?

— No, the maid was there... Except the little boy didn't go to sleep. He was just pretending. When the maid went to bed, the little boy got up and went looking for his little friends who lived next door...

— He went outside naked?

— Oh no, he got dressed. So all of these nasty little boys, who wanted to celebrate New Year's Eve like the grown-ups, came into the house. But they were out of luck, because the kitchen and dining room were locked. So what did they do?

— Tell me, what did they do?

— They went down into the garden and ate the calf.

— Raw?

— Raw, completely raw.

— Oh, what bad boys!

— Since raw veal is very hard to digest, all of those nasty little brats were very sick the next day. It's a good thing the doctor came! He gave them lots of herbal tea to drink, and they got better... But ever since then, they never gave the little boy any veal.

— And what did the little boy say?

— The little boy? Oh, he didn't give a damn.

As Good a Way as Any

A story for Guy Cros (six years old)

—Once upon a time there was an uncle and a nephew.

—Which one was the uncle?

—What do you mean, which one? The fatter one, of course!

—So uncles are fat?

—Often.

—But my Uncle Henri isn't fat.

—Your Uncle Henri isn't fat because he's an artist.

—So artists aren't fat?

—You're bothering me... If you keep interrupting, I can't tell my story.

—I won't interrupt, go ahead.

—Once upon a time there was an uncle and a nephew. The uncle was very rich, very rich.

—How much money did he have?

—Seventeen hundred billion in income, plus houses, carriages, lands...

—And horses?

—Why, of course, since he had carriages.

—And boats? Did he have boats?

—Yes, forty of them.

—Steamboats?

—Three were steamboats, and the rest had sails.

—And his nephew, did he go on the boats?

—Stop it! You won't let me tell the story.

—Go ahead, tell it, I won't bother you any more.

—The nephew, however, didn't have a sou, and that irritated him enormously.

—Why didn't his uncle give him some?

—Because his uncle was an old miser who liked to keep his money for himself. But since the nephew was his only heir...

—What's an "heir"?

—Those are the people who take your money, your furniture, everything that you own, when you're dead.

—So why didn't the nephew kill the uncle?

—Well, you're a nice one, aren't you? He didn't kill his uncle because you should never kill your uncle, under any circumstances, even for an inheritance.

—Why should you never kill your uncle?

—Because of the police.

—But what if they don't find out?

—The police always find out, the concierge tells them. And besides, you'll see that the nephew was more clever than that. He had noticed that after every meal, his uncle became quite red...

—Maybe he was drunk.

—No, it was his physical condition. He was apoplectic.

—What's "aplopecpit"?

—Apoplectic... Those are people whose blood goes to their heads, and who could die from a strong emotion.

—Am I apoplectic?

—No, and you never will be. You're not the type. So, the nephew had noticed that laughter made his uncle particularly ill, and that once he had almost died after a prolonged fit of laughter.

—Does laughter make you die?

—Yes, if you're apoplectic. One fine day, the nephew arrives at his uncle's house just as his uncle is leaving the table. Never had he eaten so well. He was as red as a rooster, and was puffing like a seal...

—Like the seals in the zoo at the Bois de Boulogne?

—No, those aren't seals, they're sea lions. The nephew says to himself, "Now's the time," and he starts to tell a funny, funny story.

—Will you tell it to me?

—Wait a moment, I'll tell it at the end... The uncle listened to the story, and he laughed, he doubled over laughing, so much that he died of laughter even before the story was finished.

—So, what was the story he told him?

—Wait a minute... Then, when the uncle was dead, they buried him, and the nephew inherited everything.

—Did he get the boats, too?

—He got everything, because he was the only heir.

—But what was the story he told his uncle?

—Why, the one I just told you.

—Which one?

—The one about the uncle and the nephew.

—You old joker!

—And what about you, eh?

The Miserable Wretch and the Good Genie

A heartbreaking story sobbed by Coquelin Cadet of the Comédie-Française

Once upon a time there was a miserable wretch... the most unfortunate there could be in the matter of miserable wretches.

Without break or respite, bad luck, frighteningly bad luck, had hounded him, such bad luck that you could not find three like it in this century, so fertile in bad luck.

...

That morning, he collected his meager resources into the pockets of his vest.

The entire amount comprised a capital of 1 fr. 90 (one franc and ninety centimes).

That was life today. And tomorrow? Miserable wretch!

So, having dabbed a little ink on the white seams of his frock coat, he went out, in the fallacious hope of *finding work.*

That frock coat, once black, had been gradually transformed by Time, the great colorist, into a green frock coat; and the miserable wretch, in all candor, now called it *my green frock coat.*

His hat, which had also been black, had turned red (apparent contradiction in the workings of Nature!).

The green frock coat and the red hat set each other off vividly.

Placed together complementarily, the green was greener, the red redder, and, in the eyes of many people, he appeared to be an eccentric chromomaniac.

...

The miserable wretch's entire day was spent in futile pursuits, in stairways ascended and descended a thousand times, in long waits in waiting rooms, in endless errands. And all without the slightest result.

Miserable wretch!

To economize on time and money, he didn't eat!

(Don't pity him; he was used to it.)

At six o'clock, unable to go on, the miserable wretch collapsed before a table in a saloon on the outer boulevards.

A fine tavern that he knew quite well, where for four sous one had the best absinthe in the neighborhood.

For four sous, to be able to *stick a little paradise under your skin,* as the late Scribe[1] said, what a joy for miserable wretches!

Ours had barely moistened his lips with the beatifying liquid, when a stranger sat at a nearby table.

The newcomer, of an unearthly beauty, contemplated, with infinite benevolence, the miserable wretch as the latter numbed his pain with little sips.

"You don't seem happy, miserable wretch?" said the stranger, in a voice so sweet that it was like the music of angels.

"Oh no... not a lot!"

"I like you, miserable wretch, and want to brighten your life. I am a good genie. Speak... What do you need to be perfectly happy?"

"I would wish for only one thing, good genie: to be assured of a hundred sous a day until the end of my existence."

"Truly, you are not a hard man to please, miserable wretch! And your wish will be granted immediately."

...

Assured of a hundred sous a day! The miserable wretch beamed.

The good genie continued.

"Only, because I have other things to do than to bring you a hundred sous every morning, and since I know the exact length of your life, I will give it to you... in one lump sum."

...

In one lump sum!

Can you see from here the face of the miserable wretch?

In one lump sum!

Not only was he assured of a hundred sous a day, but from now on he would have it... in one lump sum!

...

The good genie finished his mental calculation.

"Here: this is your tally, miserable wretch!"

And he counted out on the table 7 fr. 50 (seven francs and fifty centimes).

The miserable wretch, in turn, calculated the length of time the sum represented.

A day and a half!

Only a day and a half to live! Miserable wretch!

"Bah," he muttered, "I've seen worse!"

And, gaily pocketing his money, he set out to spend his 7 fr. 50 with chorus girls.

1. Was it really the late Scribe? (Publisher's note.)

The Gnu

for Coquelin Cadet

Are you familiar with the *gnu*?

And don't say yes, because that would be affected, or at least pretentious; for the French are ignorant not only of geography, but of natural history as well; and I only hope that the success of Zola's *Germinal* will turn more of my compatriots into naturalists.

Well, if you don't know what a gnu is, I'll tell you.

The gnu is a type of large antelope from South America, a cross between an ox, a stag, and a horse.

The gnu is not aggressive, I'm the first to admit, but it is not friendly.

Professors in the provinces have even declared, in all seriousness, that this mammal is entirely devoid of sociability.

The gnu plays an important part in certain legends in Brazil. Beware, unlucky man, of meeting the gaze of a gnu, for you will instantly go mad.

That, at least, is what is whispered on the equatorial pampas.

The legend, one day, fell under the eyes of my friend Prosper Guignard.

And what a perfect place for it to fall!

Poor Prosper Guignard was the unluckiest of men. Everything turned to failure in his hands, almost everything!

If, by chance, something did turn out well, it's curious, he found no joy in it, no satisfaction.

Happiness, for this unfortunate man, was a myth that he could not fathom.

After long reflection, and prolonged study of the most diverse philosophical systems, he finally arrived at the conclusion that on this earth, the only form of happiness is insanity.

Ah, to be mad!

Yes, but for certain people it's no easier to become mad than it is for others to remain reasonable.

Prosper Guignard tried in vain for some gentle dementia.

It was at about this time that our unfortunate friend discovered the evil reputation of the Brazilian gnu.

From then on, his path was clear, and, with an alert and hopeful step, he set out for the Jardin des Plantes.

There was indeed a gnu there, a nice fresh gnu, in a pretty little park surrounded by a pretty little fence.

Soldiers and nannies smugly contemplated the animal, unaware of the madness of Damocles suspended over their heads.

But the gnu never looked at them, occupied as it was in grazing on the low grass in its enclosure.

Prosper approached the fence, coughed, shouted, and used every strategy to attract its attention.

Annoyed, no doubt, by this indiscretion, the gnu moved to the other side, without raising its eyes.

Prosper followed the fence, rejoined the gnu, and resumed his efforts.

All day, until evening, Prosper continued this exercise, more tiring for him than for the gnu, the diameter being approximately one third of the circumference.

Fortunately, the zoo then closed.

The next day, Prosper returned in the afternoon.

Alas! No more gnu!

He questioned the guards.

"Sir," he was told, "we had to put him down this morning... We don't know what happened to him, but he went mad!"

So Prosper went mad too.

He's happy now!

To anyone who goes to see him, he cries:

"Beware of meeting my gaze!... I'm a gnu! I'm a gnu!"

An Invention

Monologue for Cadet

If anyone had ever told me that I'd invent something, I would have been very surprised! And you know... not one of those minor inventions, those little nothings... No, a serious invention.

I can't say that it's one of those inventions that galvanize the century, no, but...!

It's funny how an invention comes to you... just when you least expect it.

It's the story of Christopher Columbus and the egg!

Discovering America was the furthest thing from Columbus's mind. And then his eyes fell upon a hard-boiled egg... He said to himself: ...I don't remember what he said, but at any rate it gave him the idea to discover America.

My invention didn't happen like that.

There's no hard-boiled egg with mine.

Me, I don't claim to be anything that I'm not. I don't have a mind like lightning, but I do have a certain logic, an inexorable logic, one of those logics that is... inexorable!

Here's how I found my invention.

It was raining heavily, one of those downpours! Oh, what fine weather it was!

Next to rain like that, the universal flood would seem like a drought.

I had a number of errands to do. I found myself under the arches of the rue de Rivoli.

And I said to myself: What a pity that all of the streets in Paris aren't like the rue de Rivoli.

You would always be dry, under the arches, wherever you went. It would be charming!... If I were the government, I'd force the proprietors to build all of their houses with arches.

But perhaps that wouldn't be too liberal.

No, no arches, but what prevents shopkeepers from setting up canvas in front of their shops to shelter passers-by?

The Chamber could pass a law forcing businesses to erect tents when it rains.

Then, all of a sudden... Are you following me?... I will show you (*solemn*) the genesis of my idea... I said to myself: But why can't each citizen have his own little tent? A little piece of canvas supported by thin sticks, of bamboo for example, that you could carry yourself, over your head, to protect you from the rain.

My invention was done... All that was left was to make it practical.

This is what I imagined:

Picture to yourself a piece of cloth... silk, alpaca, whatever you like... cut into a circle, and stretched on rods made of whalebone. All of these rods are joined in the center, around a little metal ring that slides along a stick, somewhat like a cane.

When the rain stops, the rods lay against the handle, with the fabric... In that case, you can use my device as a cane.

Crack! It starts raining!... You push the little ring along the handle... the rods stretch out, and the cloth as well... You interpose this improvised shelter between you and the sky, and there you are, protected from the rain.

That's all there is to it, but you do have to think of it.

I'll bet that in three months my invention will be in everyone's hands.

You could make them in all prices, cotton for the working class, silk for the wealthy.

But it's not enough to invent something, you have to baptize your creation.

I considered words in Greek and Latin, the way they do in science. But I decided that would be pretentious.

So I said to myself: Let's see... I came up with an elegant invention, let's give it an elegant name. My device is meant to provide a little shade, so I'll call it "little shade" in Italian: umbrella.

But I'm nattering on. I'm off to the patent office; I don't want anyone to steal my idea. Because, you know, when an idea is in the air, you can't be too careful.

A White Night for a Red Hussar

Monologue for Cadet

I've always wondered why we call a night spent out of bed a white night. I just spent a night like that, and was rather... blue.

Which did not prevent my concierge, when I returned in the morning, from greeting me with a certain expression... as if to say:

"Aha, you rascal! Taking life easy, eh?"

And yet... But I'm getting ahead of myself.

I must tell you that for some time I had been in love.

Oh, in love, you know!... not to die for. But still, lightly smitten.

She was a very sweet little blonde, with little curls all over her forehead. She was always at the window when I passed.

After I'd passed a number of times, I ended by believing that she recognized me, and gave her a little smile. I even imagined—you know how we get these ideas—that she smiled back.

That was a mistake; I had proof of that later, unfortunately too late.

I said to myself, "I'll have to look into this, some day."

While waiting, I gathered information, discreetly, without seeming to.

She was married to a rather disagreeable man, apparently, the director of a large factory that made machine-guns.

The disagreeable man went out every evening at about eight, visited his club, and didn't return until late.

"Good," I said to myself, "that's all I need."

It was then around the time of Carnival.

On the occasion of this celebration, my friends had invited me to a ball—costumed, naturally.

I'm known for my imagination; so my friends said, "Try to find an amusing costume."

And so I disguised myself, that morning, as a *red hussar from Monaco*.

You may say that there are no red hussars in Monaco, that there are no hussars there at all; or that, if there are, they generally wear street clothes.

I know that as well as you; but doesn't a bit of fantasy excuse all inexactitude?

As I contemplated myself in the wardrobe mirror (my wardrobe has a mirror), I said to myself, "Say, this would be the perfect occasion to go see my little blonde. She could never refuse such a dashing red hussar."

The fact is, just between us, that I looked pretty good in that costume. Not bad at all, in fact.

I eat early... A good dinner, substantial, to give me strength, and generously fortified with wine, to give me... nerve.

I buckle my scabbard, for I have a sword, as is only right, and there I am ready for battle.

As I approach the house of my beloved, I see the husband leave.

Good, it's going well... After he's gone a bit further, I mount the stairs, quietly, because of the spurs that I'm not quite used to, and which red hussars wear rather long.

I pull the foot of a poor doe which now serves as a bell-pull.

A footstep is heard behind the door. The door opens... There she is... my little blonde. I say to her: ....

In fact, what could I have said to her?

Because, you know, in such moments, you say whatever pops

into your head, and then, five minutes later, you'll be hanged if you can repeat it.

But what I do remember perfectly is what she answered, in a furious tone: "You're mad, sir!... And my husband is coming back... I hear him now."

And bang! She slams the door in my face.

In fact, someone was indeed climbing the stairs with a heavy step, the terrible step of the pitiless husband.

As much of a red hussar as I was, I'll admit that I was nervous.

There was a simple way to resolve the situation, you'll tell me. Just go down the stairs and leave, that's all. But, as an English philosopher once wisely observed, the simplest ideas come last.

I thought of everything, except leaving.

For a moment, I thought that I should draw my sword, and resolutely await the husband.

"Absurd," I said to myself, "and compromising."

And the man kept climbing the stairs.

All of a sudden, I see a little door, which I hadn't noticed at first because it was painted to look like marble, like the rest of the hall. But what funny marble! Real Carnival marble!

At a moment like that, there's no time to waste on frivolous esthetics.

I open the door, and rush in desperately, without even noticing where I was.

Just in time! The husband was at the top of the stairs.

I hear the grinding of a key in a lock, a door opening, a door closing—probably the same one—and finally I can breathe.

Only then do I think of examining the room that had been my salvation.

You will never guess the curious place into which I'd stuffed myself.

You smile... so you've guessed!

Yes, it was there... or rather, HERE!

Gently, without a sound, I lift the latch and push the door... It resists.

I push a little harder... It still resists.

I push very hard, with superhuman force. The door still resists, like a door which has serious reasons not to open.

I say to myself, "The wood is swollen from the humidity." I brace myself against the... thing there, and... ugh! A wasted effort.

This is, decidedly, some solid carpentry.

An infernal idea crosses my mind... What if the husband, seeing me from below, and guessing my wicked plans, had shut me in there, thanks to a lock on the outside!

What a situation for a red hussar!

On a Carnival night! And I'm expected at the ball!

No, no, it's not possible. I dismiss this sinister thought.

And yet the door remains as unmovable as a rock.

Tired of the struggle, I sit down—fortunately, you can sit in such places—and wait. Damn! Someone will soon come to my rescue.

They don't come quickly. In fact, they don't come at all.

What then do they eat in this building?

Quince jelly, I suppose.

From the street, there rise to my ears the joyful clamor of trumpets, hunting horns, bugles, and then—terrible!—the sound of clocks, every quarter hour, every half hour, every hour...!

And my anticipated liberator doesn't come. Did everyone gorge himself on bismuth that day?

The next time I visit this building, I'll send every tenant a melon.

From time to time, with touching despair, I stand up, and, calling upon all my strength, I push the door, I push, I push!

Ah! For a strong door, it's a good strong door!

Finally, exhausted, I give up. The handle of my sword is digging into my ribs. I hang it on the latch and fall asleep. A restless sleep, punctuated with nightmares. The sounds from the street die down, bit by bit. I hear only a single stubborn horn, calling heroically in the distance.

Then the horn goes to bed, like everyone else...

    .....

I awake!... It's already early morning. I rub my eyes, and remember everything. My red hussar's heart leaps to my mouth. In a rage, I unhook my sword and pull it to me...

    .....

I dare not tell you the rest.

What an imbecile I was! Double imbecile! Triple imbecile! Hundredfold idiot! Thousandfold cretin! I had spent the night pushing the door...

It opened inward!

A Luminous Idea

Monologue performed by Coquelin Cadet of the Comédie-Française

This morning, I received a visit from an amusing character... an inventor!

Do you like inventors? Me, I adore them, even if they don't invent anything, which is the case with practically all inventors.

I like their obsession, the fire in their eyes, their disheveled appearance. As for obsession and fire in the eyes, my man was in the grand tradition, but it was especially in the matter of slovenly attire that he exceeded all that I'd seen before.

In particular, a button on his coat inserted, as if by chance, into a buttonhole on his vest, and reciprocally.

It was rather picturesque.

...

I was shaving before the mirror (I shave myself, now).

The man blew in like a hurricane.

"Hello," he said. "How are you?"

"No worse than yesterday," I replied. "And yourself?"

"Do you recognize me?"

"Me? Not at all."

"Ah! I was about to say, it's because I have a beard now... And besides, you've never seen me before."

Without reminding the man that, strictly speaking, the second reason sufficed, I asked the object of his visit.

"I am an inventor, sir," he answered proudly.

"Ah! Heavens, I'd already guessed."

"I come to you because you are a man who is intelligent, well educated, and cares nothing for money, where a good idea is concerned."

I bowed.

I am, in fact, intelligent and well educated; and when an idea strikes me as practical, ingenious, or simply bizarre, I will not hesitate to sacrifice a million or two to realize it.

Brusquely, the man continued:

"Which do you prefer... to burn or to rot?"

"Excuse me," I said, a bit startled, "to rot?"

"Or to burn. Well, answer me."

"My God, sir, the idea of rotting is in no way particularly seductive. As for burning, may I confess that I am not irresistibly drawn to it, at the moment?"

"At the moment, yes, but when you're dead?"

"Oh! When I'm dead!"

And I sketched a gesture of utter indifference.

My inventor continued, in a rather vulgar tone:

"Yes, rotting in the ground is really disgusting, but being burned isn't much nicer."

"However..."

"There is no however. I have invented a process that makes cremation and burial obsolete. I replace all that with *inaeration*! Eh? *Inaeration*!"

"That's not a foolish idea."

"Don't mock me before you learn more."

"I assure you, sir..."

"Drop it. You're dead, right?"

"Just a minute!"

"It's just a supposition. You're dead, they bring me your body, I put it in my oven..."

"But that's cremation."

"Imbecile! I put it in my oven, a special oven of my own invention, and I desiccate it. I desiccate it. Do you understand? I DESICCATE it. I do not cook it, I do not roast it, I do not burn it, I DES-IC-CATE IT. That is to say that I rid it of all the water that it contains by evaporation... Do you know the approximate proportion of water in the human body?"

"I admit that I..."

"Well, it's about eighty per cent, four fifths."

"That much?"

"Yes sir, that much. So General Boulanger, whom you worship so..."

"But I never said..."

"Don't interrupt... General Boulanger, whom you worship so, weighs eighty-two kilograms; therefore he represents roughly sixty-five kilograms of water. So, for every eighty-two times that you cry "Hooray for Boulanger," you should count sixty-five for pure water. So much for human importance! And Francisque Sarcey, then! Do you know Sarcey?"

"I know him without knowing him. Sometimes in the morning, as I walk along Douai Street, I see him shaking a scatter rug out the window, but you can't call that knowing a man."

"Well, it's frightening how much water Sarcey contains. I can't give you the exact number, you'd think I was joking. On the other hand, there are some individuals who offer very little excess. Sarah Bernhardt, for example, there's a temperament that's truly... What's the word?"

"Dramatic?"

"No, *anhydrous*."

"Materialist!"

"Are you married?"

"Not at the moment."

"Do you have a mistress?"

"Mistress would be an exaggeration, but I have a sweet little girlfriend."

"How much does she weigh?"

"My word, I never weighed her, but I can tell you approximately... Let's see, she's not too big, probably about fifty kilos."

"Well, let me tell you that the object of your idolatry contains about forty kilos of water."

"Stop it, you disgust me!"

"Forty liters of water! You hear me... *eighty pints*!"

And the inventor pronounced the words "eighty pints" in a tone of indescribable contempt. And what had I ever done to him?

He continued point-blank:

"But you're just wasting my time with this business about your girlfriend. Let me return to my invention: Once your body is entirely desiccated, I soak it in a liquid of my own composition, based on nitric acid, which transforms it into an explosive material similar to guncotton. Then, all you do is ignite it... Pfff... fff... ttt! A flash of light, a great cloud of white smoke rises to the sky, and all is said and done! What do you think of my idea?"

"It's luminous."

"But that's not all. Instead of transforming your body into a simple explosive, I can create a complete fireworks display: firecrackers, Roman candles, rockets, Catherine wheels, etc., etc. For poor families, I can transform, for only thirty francs, the dear departed into Roman candles of all colors. For ten thousand francs, I can produce a first class display with an allegorical bouquet."

"Superb!"

"Better yet... Old soldiers could will their mortal remains, transformed in this way, to the artillery. They could be loaded into shells or cannons. What a joy, ten years after your death, to shoot the enemies of France! Doesn't that tempt you?"

"Yes, it's an inviting proposition, but as far as my personal body is concerned, I prefer to wait."

The inventor took his hat and stormed out, furious.

What do you want? I'm in no hurry.

The Doctor

Monologue for Cadet

For sheer nerve, there's nobody like a doctor. Infernal nerve! And contempt for human life, as well!

You're sick, your doctor comes. He palpates you, he auscultates you, he interrogates you, all while thinking of something else. Once his prescription is written, he says, "I'll return," and—you can be sure of it—that he will, once you've passed the point of *no* return.

When you die, an undertaker comes at once to bring him a little kickback for the funeral.

If you prove resistant to the illness, and especially to his prescriptions, the doctor rubs his hands, because his little visits, and his cut from the pharmacist in particular, start to snowball, and become quite a tidy sum.

Only one thing bothers the good doctor: that's when you get well quickly. Even then, he finds a way to work his mischief, and says, with infernal aplomb:

"Aha! I pulled you out of that one!"

But the doctor who has the most nerve of all is mine; or rather ex-mine, because I got rid of him, and, believe me, I didn't regret it.

After I had been too cold and then too hot—or too hot and then too cold, I don't remember—I became somewhat indisposed. Hoping to save my skin—what do you expect, it's the only one I have—I called my doctor, who arrived promptly.

I was already feeling bad, but after his first prescription, I took a definite turn for the worse, and had to stay in bed.

Another visit, another prescription, another downturn.

In short, after four days, I'd lost several pounds... even kilos.

One morning when I was feeling not at all well, my doctor, after auscultating me more carefully than usual, asked me:

"Are you content with this apartment?"

"Why, yes, pretty much."

"How much is your rent?"

"Three thousand and four."

"Is the concierge acceptable?"

"I've never had any complaints."

"And the landlord?"

"The landlord is very nice."

"Do the chimneys smoke?"

"Not much."

Etc., etc.

And I wondered, "What is this character driving at?" Whether my apartment is humid or not, that might have some bearing on my illness, but how much rent I pay? What does that have to do with him? And despite my weakened condition, I ventured to ask:

"But doctor, why all of these questions?"

"I'll tell you," he replied. "I'm looking for an apartment, and yours would suit me perfectly."

"But... I have no plans to move!"

"And yet you'll have to in a few days."

"To move?"

"Something like that."

And I understood!

My doctor considered my condition serious, and made that rather clear.

I can't express the effect of this sudden revelation, not in any language.

Terrible anxiety at first, stark terror!

And then, white-hot rage! You don't act like that with a sick man, with a client, and a good client, I must say.

Ah! You want my apartment, my friend? Well, nothing doing!

.....

The next time you're sick, let me recommend this procedure: get angry. For you, it might make you worse. For me, it cured me.

I kicked my doctor out the door.

I threw my medications out the window.

When I say that I threw them out the window, I exaggerate. I don't like to break glass on purpose; it could hurt people walking by, and I don't want to hurt people: I'm no doctor!

I contented myself with sending all my bottles back to the pharmacist, with a stern note.

There were so many bottles, so many packets and boxes!

There were so many, that one day I made a mistake: I put syrup on my stomach, and swallowed a plaster.

In fact, it was the only time I got any relief.

After that, I renewed my lease, and never consulted a doctor again.

A Malcontent

Monologue performed by Coquelin Cadet

That man on the sidewalk, waiting for the Batignolles-Clichy-Odéon bus, at the same time as me, I was sure that I knew him, but where had I seen him, and what was his name? Cruel enigma!

Although not a young man, he was a man who was still young.

His features, his mannerisms, his entire appearance, indicated someone who was restless, touchy, and ill-tempered.

The bus finally arrived.

As the numbers were called, the crowd surged forward, splashing through the mud that covered Paris, that day, with a fluid and unusually copious mantle.

7, 8, and 9 boarded.

The man who was still young, bearing number 10, grumbled words of disappointment that ended with the cry "Hooray for Boulanger!"

"Well, good," I thought, "a malcontent!"

Another wait, another bus, another splashing.

This time, we were able to climb onto the platform, my provisional stranger and I.

I paid my fare with three bronze centimes.

The man did the same with the help of a two franc coin, upon which the conductor gave him the sum of one franc and seventy centimes, composed entirely of small change.

"What do you expect me to do with all of this grapeshot?" the man cried in exasperation.

"I'm terribly sorry," the conductor replied, with a courtesy one seldom encounters in that class of functionaries, "but I have no larger coins in my pouch."

Still grumbling, the man distributed his thirty-four sous into different pockets, and emitted a second cry of "Hooray for Boulanger!"

At that moment, he noticed me, recognized me, and shook my hand with all the outward signs of the greatest pleasure.

"I'm sure that you don't recognize me," he said.

"I do, but I don't really remember..."

"I might have guessed. It only happens to me. I recognize all my friends, and none of my friends recognizes me. Hooray for Boulanger!"

He decided to give his name: Fortuné Bidard. I instantly remembered my old school chum.

Fortuné Bidard! If ever a name went poorly with a personality, it was his.

From earliest childhood, life for him had been nothing but a perpetual harvest of misfortunes, a forest of gaffes, a hurricane of undeserved punishment.

Every day was marked by an unfortunate episode befalling Bidard in class, in the street, or in his family.

An excellent student, he never won the smallest prize, and was never awarded the slightest certificate.

It was as if a legion of evil little demons swarmed around Fortuné, plotting to ruin his every move.

One adventure, among others:

One day, we were given a test in mathematics for an important competition. Fortuné worked with concentration, mixed with joy. It was evidently going well.

Suddenly, Bidard mopped his brow, and rubbed his hands in utter satisfaction.

"Are you done?" I asked in a low voice.

"Yes, I just have to copy it out... It's wonderful, my friend, I didn't miss a problem."

Then, before he recopied his paper, he raised his right arm and snapped his fingers. The proctor understood, and agreed.

Bidard's absence was brief.

He hurried back, adjusting his suspenders, returned to his seat, and let out a cry of horror that went straight to our hearts.

Among the papers he had taken, you know where, were the problems he had worked so successfully.

Try to find them now! Of course, there was no time to redo them, and, once again, a pretty prize in mathematics slipped through his fingers.

Unfortunate Fortuné! He told me that luck had continued to turn its back to him with the same persistence.

"Nothing succeeded for me, my poor friend. I worked like a slave, and had all the trouble in the world to pass my exams. And you want me to be content? Bah! Hooray for Boulanger!"

"Hooray for Boulanger!"

"And women, too! More success on my part! I won't tell you about my first experiences with women, it would make your hair stand on end. But recently, I had a little girlfriend, very nice, very sweet, and whom I thought was faithful. Her name was Caroline. One day, I arrived alone at the cafe where we usually went together, Caroline and I. One of my friends asked, "What have you done with Caroline?" I don't what came over me, but I thought I'd make a joke, so I answered, "Caroline? I dumped her!" At that, he shook my hand and said, "Well, old fellow, congratulations on getting rid of the little slut, who slept with all of your friends, except the ones who weren't interested."

I asked around: it was true. And you want me to be content? Bah! Hooray for Boulanger!"

"Hooray for Boulanger!"

"But I must leave you... Just imagine, I'm making my first call on my fiancée, a charming individual, the daughter of a shopkeeper on rue de Richelieu ... I don't know why, but I have a feeling that something will happen between now and then. We're almost there. Here's my stop. Goodbye!"

"Goodbye!"

Fortuné Bidard shook my hand, and went down the steps.

He went further down than he expected, for I saw him flat on the ground, which (as I already told you) was covered with a pretty coat of very thick, very black, and very abundant mud.

Bridard stood up in a rage, and even as the bus arrived at the National Library, I could still hear his cries of "Hooray for Boulanger!"

"Hooray for Boulanger," I echoed, with a note of pity.

Untitled

"Due to a sentiment that all will understand, and that must, for once, be lauded, the Board of Censors has forbidden the representation upon the stage of officers of the peace, and of those scenes we have often seen in revues."

THE CENSOR: Ah, good day, sir! You brought your revue?... And it's called?...

THE AUTHOR: *We Are Not Cattle.*

THE CENSOR: *We Are Not Cattle!...* And do you think we'll permit that title? Why, you're proclaiming the right to idleness! The title alone is a call to anarchy. *(Crossing out the title with a thick blue pencil.)* Change that title for us!

THE AUTHOR: Very well, sir.

THE CENSOR: *(Leafing through the manuscript.)* Huh! What do I see in the first act? A chorus of policemen! I suppose you haven't heard about the attack on rue des Bons-Enfants.

THE AUTHOR: I beg your pardon, but...

THE CENSOR: *(Crossing it out.)* No, no, no policemen! If we let you have your way, you revue writers, in three months there wouldn't be a single police station left in Paris!

THE AUTHOR: I just...

THE CENSOR: *(Continuing.)* And this? A song called "It Wouldn't Hurt To Have Dessert"? Thought you'd glorify deserters, eh? *(He crosses it out.)*

THE AUTHOR: But I can assure you...

THE CENSOR: Soldiers now! At the very moment that a handful of French troops are, without hesitation, shedding their blood in Dahomey! Sir, your patriotic fiber is singularly atrophied!

THE AUTHOR: Ah, I'm sorry!

THE CENSOR: Now we come to the second act. As the curtain rises, I read, "A clock strikes twelve." Strikes! No, that will not be tolerated! Strikes, indeed! Sir, don't you think that the miners' strikes in Carmaux are still too fresh in the public's mind to evoke them here?

THE AUTHOR: See here, sir...

THE CENSOR: *(Pitilessly eliminating the entire second act.)* No, no strikes!... Ah, here's a "Parisian Roundelay." If you don't mind, we'll put that off until next year.

THE AUTHOR: *(Somewhat bewildered.)* ???

THE CENSOR: *(Crossing out the "Parisian Roundelay.")* The murder on rue de Botzaris is still too recent, and the unfortunate victim not yet identified. How do we know that she wasn't Parisian? Do you know something about it?

THE AUTHOR: My word, no.

THE CENSOR: Well, then! And isn't the "Parisian Roundelay" followed by a chorus about a girl from the country?

THE AUTHOR: That wasn't indicated.

THE CENSOR: And a good thing for you that it wasn't! The victim at rue de Botzaris might well have come from one of the departments. I would have suppressed those lines.

(The scene continues. At the end, the author rises, collects his manuscript, and withdraws, overcome by torpor.)

At the Publisher

A true story.

CHARACTERS:

LOYS LAZUR: *a slightly obsessive young poet.*

DUCONNEL: *an illiterate but greedy publisher.*

DUCONNEL: Ah, there you are, my friend; please, have a seat...

LAZUR: (*Sits.*)

DUCONNEL: Well, I had someone read your little thing. You have talent, it seems. I think we'll print this.

LAZUR: ...

DUCONNEL: Now, where the devil did I stick your manuscript? Ah, here it is. *The Surveyor's Daughter-in-law*, is that it?

LAZUR: (*A bit annoyed.*) I don't think so.

DUCONNEL: No, my mistake. This is yours: *Eagles and Doves, Sonnets.*

LAZUR: Exactly.

DUCONNEL: May I make a little observation?

LAZUR: Why, of course.

DUCONNEL: There's one thing that bothers me about your manuscript, and that's that all of the poems aren't the same width.

LAZUR: (*A bit bewildered.*) ????

DUCONNEL: Yes, they're all the same length, but not the same width. Look, this one takes up the whole page, and this one barely half.

LAZUR: Well, of course! The first has twelve syllables to a line, and the second has six.

DUCONNEL: I don't deny that, but I can assure you that it won't appeal to the eye. Can you fix it by Monday?

LAZUR: (*Gesturing in despair.*) You have no idea!

DUCONNEL: Never mind, then... Now, for our terms... Are you familiar with the company's terms?

LAZUR: (*Wary.*) No.

DUCONNEL: Well, here they are. You pay for the publication. Then, if it sells, we give you two sous a copy.

LAZUR: (*Astonished.*) Oh?

DUCONNEL: Yes. These are the terms I give all new writers, and they're usually satisfied with them.

LAZUR: (*Completely discouraged.*) Oh.

DUCONNEL: Yes... Oh, I forgot something. There are a few expressions in your poems that I'd like to see you replace... For example, here's a piece that begins with "The panderers"... Couldn't you find another word that means the same thing and has...

LAZUR: ...Has the same number of syllables.

DUCONNEL: Exactly!

LAZUR: (*Rising coldly.*) Why, my dear sir, nothing could be easier... Just change it to "The publishers"...

Eight Days Later

I

—Well, if it isn't my excellent Schozanler! How are you, old top?

—Better than I can say, and happy, my poor friend, happy!

—When you're done with your happiness, don't throw it out, eh? Think of me!

—If you only knew her!

—Ah, there's some creature, then?

—Please, my friend, don't use that word about her.

—Damn, you worry me!

—I only met her yesterday.

—And in what chicken coop did you dig up this pearl? In the Jardin de Paris?

—(*Severely.*) I would appreciate it, my friend, when you speak of this person, to employ a different tone.

—Fine, fine, your princess will be respected.

—When I met her, my friend, she was as pure as the angel of creation.

—Very nice!... But are you sure of that?

—Next to her, Joan of Arc was a shameless hussy!

—You do well, you, when it comes to girlfriends... Care for a drink?

—If you like.

—Waiter!... What will you have?

—Spearmint.

—Aha! And a beer for me. Waiter!... a beer and a spearmint!

(*After a drink, I leave my friend, shaking his hand with a twinge of envy.*)

II

The next week:

—Well, if it isn't my excellent Schozanler! How are you, old top?

—Thank you, my friend, not too well.

—What's wrong?

—Nothing, really. I'm just not doing well, that's all.

—And your radiant angel?

—Do me a favor, will you?... Never mention that cow.

—But Joan of Arc, who...

—Don't drag the noble figure of Joan of Arc, one of the purest in our history, into this sordid escapade.

—The truth is that you look pretty glum.

—Oh, I'll get over it... Care for a drink?

—Gladly.

—Waiter!...What will you have?

—A beer.

—And a hot gum syrup for me. Waiter!... a beer and a hot gum syrup!

(*After a drink, I leave my friend, shaking his hand without a twinge of envy.*)

Magnum's Revenge

(Pantomimette for La Nouvelle Cirque)

CHARACTERS:

MAGNUM, *a young dog who is very small, very small, but excessively mangy and wily.*

BLACK, *a large middle-aged Newfoundland, not very clever, but an excellent companion.*

ROSE SWEET, *a desiccated shrewish old woman, owner of a little cottage for rent.*

I. In a moment of forgetfulness, the young dog Magnum soils Rose Sweet's cottage door.

II. She, returning from the market at that very moment, punishes the guilty party with a bony and excessive hand.

III. Magnum withdraws, his dignity and mortified flesh aflame. The state of his soul consists entirely of pondering, "What nasty trick can I play on the old hag?"

IV. Suddenly, he strikes his little head with his little paw, and utters a joyful bark, which corresponds almost exactly to the *eureka* of the ancient Greeks.

V. And then he is off at top speed in a familiar direction!

VI. Soon, he returns accompanied by Black, a large white Newfoundland of his acquaintance.

VII. En route, Magnum explains to Black, with some care, his role in the enterprise.

VIII. Docilely, Black positions himself by the cottage door, holding his good doggy's head high.

IX. Little Magnum, anticipatory joy in his eyes, jumps onto Black's back, and from there onto his head.

X. Having reached the proper height, he presses his cute little paw to the electric button at the cottage door.

XI. Dring, dring, dring, dring, dring, dring...

XII. As the last *drings* are still echoing, the scene is transformed with the rapidity of a lightning bolt thrown by an expert hand.

XIII. Magnum jumps to the ground, and goes to lie on the sidewalk, a few yards upstream of the cottage.

XIV. The same with Black. Only for him, it's downstream.

XV. Meanwhile, Rose Sweet, eager for possible tenants, rushes to the door, wiping her hands, soiled with potato peelings, on her apron, as she vainly strives to twist her morose and naturally aggressive features into an exquisite smile of welcome.

XVI. Nobody at the cottage door! Nobody on the avenue! On the horizon, not even the shadow of a naughty little boy! What, then?

XVII. The only living creatures are two dogs, sunning themselves. They didn't ring, that's obvious! Not that big Newfoundland, not that minuscule mutt, no! What, then?

XVIII. Rose Sweet shuts the cottage door, and returns inside, attributing the disturbance to some phenomenon of auditory hallucination.

XIX. No sooner has Rose Sweet retreated, than the two dogs reinitiate the little strategy outlined in numbers VIII, IX, X, XI, XII, XIII, and XIV.

XX. Rose Sweet renews the activity meticulously described in numbers XV, XVI, and XVII.

XXI. But the hypothesis of a phenomenon of auditory hallucination no longer satisfies her.

XXII. It's *ghosts*, perhaps! Indescribable terror on the part of the hateful crone!

XXIII. Yes, that must be it, *ghosts*! The souls of former tenants that she had tormented, who have come to torment her in turn!

XXIV, XXV, etc., etc., N. The little game continues, until the audience shows obvious signs of lassitude.

N + 1. Driven insane, Rose Sweet hangs herself in the garden, on the branch of a Bartlett pear tree.

N + 2. And Rose Sweet was such a peevish old lady, and so disagreeable, that nobody comes to her funeral...

N + 3. ...Except Magnum and Black, who are laughing fit to kill—which, in a way, they did.

Tonton in Society

(Tonton, six years old, is visiting Madame Durand with his mother and father. An unbearable child, he has found the button that controls the electric lights in the salon, and amuses himself by producing, in turn, darkness and light.)

PAPA: Settle down, Tonton, or I will have to become angry.

TONTON: (*Continuing his game.*) Day... Night... Day... Night... I've never seen anything more fun than this.

PAPA: You'll be less amused by the spanking you'll get if you continue.

TONTON: Probably!... Still, it's handy to have one little button that you turn for the light!... Why don't we have one like this at our house?

PAPA: Because we don't have electricity at our house.

TONTON: Well, shoot, let's get the stuff, then! Madame Durand has it, why can't we?... Madame Durand's not smarter than us, after all...

(Tonton receives a sharp reprimand, reminding him of the value of social conventions, but the subject of electricity continues to fascinate him.)

TONTON: So, elec... elec...

PAPA: Electricity.

TONTON: Yes, electrixity, so it's not something like gas? It doesn't come through pipes?

PAPA: No, my friend.

TONTON: What does it come through, then?

PAPA: It would take too long to explain. You'll learn about it in school.

TONTON: You learn that in school? Do you learn how to clean chimneys, too?

PAPA: What?... To clean chimneys? You're crazy!

TONTON: Sure! If you learn stuff about light, you could learn things about heat too!

(Stunned by this childish logic, the father has no answer. He consults his watch, and suggests a departure.)

PAPA: (*To the mother.*) If you like, dear, we can leave now. We're having dinner with your mother. And you know that if we're the least bit tardy, she gives us a rather cool reception.

TONTON: Say, papa?

PAPA: What, my friend?

TONTON: When grandma complains, why don't you give her a drop of oil?

PAPA: (*Baffled.*) A drop of oil?

TONTON: Yes, like you did the other day for the lock. (*He doubles over.*)

(They take their leave of Madame Durand. Tonton takes advantage of this interlude to indulge in enthusiastic nasal explorations in the worst possible taste. His papa notices.)

PAPA: (*Indignant.*) Do you want me to help you, you scoundrel?

TONTON: You couldn't, your fingers are too fat.

PAPA: It's disgusting, my friend, to pull crusts from your nose like that.

TONTON: (*Coldly.*) Fine, I'll put them back.

The Playwright and the Director, or One Year Later

THE PLAYWRIGHT: Well then, my dear director, have you familiarized yourself with my little manuscript?

THE DIRECTOR: Perfectly, my friend, perfectly!

THE PLAYWRIGHT: And?

THE DIRECTOR: I like your play very much; I've decided to schedule it soon.

THE PLAYWRIGHT: Ah! (*Incontestable satisfaction suffuses his features.*)

THE DIRECTOR: Except, may I request one little change?

THE PLAYWRIGHT: (*Only too happy.*) But of course!

THE DIRECTOR: There's a mother-in-law in your play, a mother-in-law whom you paint in the somber colors with which, for far too long, these old women have been depicted.

THE PLAYWRIGHT: But...

THE DIRECTOR: That's not done any more, my friend. Let's leave that kind of pleasantry to the cabaret, to the ignominious cabaret. Believe me, mothers-in-law are just women like everybody else, no better, no worse.

THE PLAYWRIGHT: But eliminating the role will ruin my whole play.

THE DIRECTOR: Not at all, my friend, not at all! Instead of a mother-in-law, you just substitute an old aunt, that's all.

THE PLAYWRIGHT: Agreed!

ONE YEAR LATER

(The young playwright's play was performed to great success. Encouraged, he has submitted a second manuscript to his director. He comes for the reply.)

THE PLAYWRIGHT: Well then, my dear director, have you familiarized yourself with my little manuscript?

THE DIRECTOR: Perfectly, my friend, perfectly!

THE PLAYWRIGHT: And?

THE DIRECTOR: I like your play very much; I've decided to schedule it soon.

THE PLAYWRIGHT: Ah! (*Incontestable satisfaction suffuses his features.*)

THE DIRECTOR: Except, may I request one little change?

THE PLAYWRIGHT: (*Only too happy.*) But of course!

THE DIRECTOR: There's a cousin in your play, a disagreeable, indiscreet, and quarrelsome old woman. What if, instead of a cousin, we made her a mother-in-law?

THE PLAYWRIGHT: (*Somewhat surprised.*) But you yourself, my dear director, told me last year...

THE DIRECTOR: Last year, my poor friend, I wasn't married!

THE PLAYWRIGHT: Well, yes, but...

THE DIRECTOR: (*Taking his hand.*) Please, do it for me. And to make it funnier (*with a tiger's snarl*), let's bump her off in the first act!

THE PLAYWRIGHT: Agreed!

Official Rehabilitation

THE JUDGE: Do you still claim your innocence?

THE VICTIM OF A JUDICIAL ERROR: More than ever, your honor.

THE JUDGE: And the most bizarre thing about the whole business is that you're right... The court in Rouen dealt you a bad hand.

THE VICTIM: Since my sentencing, I have not let a day pass without protesting my innocence.

THE JUDGE: You even irritated your guards, it appears, with your incessant yammering.

THE VICTIM: Maybe you think it's amusing to be imprisoned when you did nothing!

THE JUDGE: Did nothing, did nothing... that's easily said. You didn't murder your wife, I'll grant you that, but you have other misdeeds on your conscience. I see from your dossier that in 1880, you were ticketed for having no light on your car from 8:30 to 9:00 in the evening.

THE VICTIM: Yes, I remember.

THE JUDGE: Oh, you remember... that's good! Besides, you have lived, matrimonially, for close to a year with a certain Marie Dézomard, a seamstress at Yvetot... How do you expect, with such a record, that the experts not find you guilty of *poisoning with an unknown poison*?

THE VICTIM: Those gentlemen should have paid more attention to the case.

THE JUDGE: (*Severe.*) You forget that those gentlemen have other things to do than to think about you. Mr. Cerné has his classes at the medical school in Rouen. Mr. Pennetier cannot neglect his museum. As for the subtle (as his name indicates) chemist Mr. Fox, the municipal laboratory summons him with a clarion call.

THE VICTIM: I don't deny it, your honor, but do you think I had nothing better to do than spend ten years over there?

THE JUDGE: (*Indulgent.*) I concede your point. And so the government, resolved to set things right, will grant you compensation.

THE VICTIM: Ah!

THE JUDGE: Yes... Your lawyer is asking for 100,000 francs, which would give you 10,000 francs for each year of prison. That's excessive!... 10,000 francs a year? Many honorable functionaries don't make that much! We will award you 20,000 francs.

THE VICTIM: That's not enough.

THE JUDGE: From those 20,000 francs, the government expects, as is only just, to deduct all of the expenses that you incurred: for your round trip to Melanesia, 1,000 francs...

THE VICTIM: You're going to make me pay for the trip to Nouméa?

THE JUDGE: Oh, but so little! 1,000 francs! Come now, be reasonable, and admit that few agencies would transport you that far for such a trifling sum. As for living expenses there, food, lodging, and clothing, we'll charge you 1,200 francs a year, that is, 12,000 francs for your entire stay in New Caledonia. You must agree that it's a bargain.

THE VICTIM: (*Energetic.*) Never!

THE JUDGE: Oh, you!... When will you ever agree to anything!... That leaves you a sum of 7,000 francs, which will be remitted to you after the necessary formalities. Above all, don't forget to get your receipt stamped.

THE VICTIM: (*Discouraged.*) I'll remember, your honor.

THE JUDGE: Now that you're rehabilitated, you are excused, and may this little adventure serve as a lesson to you.

A Scrupulous Woman

HE: (*Crushed with sorrow.*) So then, you cheat on me.

SHE: (*Perfectly calm, and not flustered for a sou.*) I cheat on you.

HE: And with whom, good God! With an old man!

SHE: A repulsive old man.

HE: Ugly!

SHE: One could say hideous.

HE: And stupid.

SHE: A fool.

HE: But then... Why? Why?

SHE: If I told you, you wouldn't believe me. You'd accuse me of boasting.

HE: Speak!

SHE: What's the use?

HE: I want to know everything... I have the right.

SHE: (*Without batting an eye.*) Oh, your right!

HE: Speak, I beg of you... Maybe I can pardon you...

SHE: I don't need your pardon. My conscience doesn't bother me... on the contrary.

HE: (*Sarcastically.*) On the contrary?

SHE: Absolutely!... But because you insist, I'll tell you everything. I granted my supreme favors to that disgusting old man for money.

HE: (*Pouncing like a Bengal tiger.*) For money!... And you say that without blushing!... For money!

SHE: (*Coldly.*) For cash, if you prefer.

HE: Wretched woman!... Cheating on me for money!... And have

I ever refused you money?... Haven't I granted your every wish?... Have you ever asked for a sou that I've denied you?

SHE: Never, my poor friend! I'm the first to recognize that your generosity has been above reproach.

HE: Why, then?

SHE: Don't get upset. Soon you'll fall at my feet.

HE: I'm listening.

SHE: In addition to this elderly lover that you just discovered, I have another: this one young, handsome, and amusing! A gem of a man, but unfortunately as poor as Job. As poor as Job, that is, before the invention of cigarette papers.

HE: You have the effrontery to joke!

SHE: (*Lightly.*) One has to laugh!... So, since I didn't want my poor sweetheart to do without anything, and (*solemn and dignified*) since I refused to touch a single centime of our household budget for this little escapade...

HE: (*Taking her in his arms.*) I understand perfectly, and you're an angel!

SHE: And you, a gallant gentleman with whom it is a pleasure to discuss matters!

.....

As seldom occurs in our daily life, this conclusion has the benefit of making four people happy at the same time. And isn't that better than going to the cafe?

Silvérie, or The Dutch Fund

CHARACTERS:
VICTOR DODEAU.
MUCHE, *his friend.*
SILVÉRIE.
A BELLBOY.

(The scene is a hotel room. A small table with drawers, downstage right; a chair to the left of the table. Two other chairs, downstage left. A door upstage. A fireplace, seen from the side, upstage right. On the fireplace, a clock.)

SCENE I
VICTOR DODEAU, *alone.*

DODEAU: (*The clock strikes eight, which he counts on his fingers.*) Two-thirty... Today at exactly four o'clock, my pecuniary situation will change completely. The passive won't diminish, obviously... The passive never diminishes... But the active will increase by twenty-five louis that owe nothing to anyone... That is, they'll pay nothing to anyone... Which amounts to the same thing. I will possess in all five hundred and twenty-eight francs... I'm in a very good mood... It's curious how money can help you endure poverty... Those twenty-five louis came to me absolutely out of the blue... I'm not one of those who think that if you open your mouth, roast larks will fall... No, but all the same, I do open my mouth now and then... Besides, the heavens above can give me a bit of help, since I do help myself as much as I can. Let it rain, let it blow, let it hail, I still play Manille ten hours a day... In that way, I assure a mediocre living for myself, and for my girlfriend... It's a curious story about those twenty-five louis... But someone's here...

SCENE II
MUCHE, DODEAU

MUCHE: (*Entering.*) Hello.

DODEAU: Listen, Muche. You didn't come here planning to borrow money, did you? You're not gripped by a pressing need?

MUCHE: Not at the moment. But why?

DODEAU: Is it firmly established that you didn't lose a large sum tonight? And that you have no plans to blow out your brains?

MUCHE: What are you driving at?

DODEAU: So, I can speak freely. Know then, Muche, old friend, that I am about to come into five hundred francs.

MUCHE: (*Reaching into his inside jacket pocket.*) You know, as a matter of fact...

DODEAU: (*Stopping him.*) Too late. I am about to come into twenty-five louis.

MUCHE: How?

DODEAU: I'll tell you all about it. (*They sit on the chairs at left.*) Two weeks ago, I attended a banquet for former students who had been expelled from the schools of Paris. I was admitted by special permission, since I had only been expelled from schools in the provinces. I was introduced to a wealthy Dutchman, named Van Heitner; this Dutchman, after a few drinks, expounded on the fidelity of French women, with a few remarks of unparalleled cynicism. That this coarse-haired foreigner would offer such remarks, there was nothing surprising about that. But that he could so express himself before a group of young Frenchmen, each of whom had at least one, if not two, mistresses to defend, that went too far... I leapt up with a bound (*he rises*), a single bound... We had been drinking freely, as I said, both wine and liquor, and I could feel my face aflame with alcohol and rage. (*Gravely.*) I looked that Dutchman right in the yellow of his eyes... and in a moment of silence... of deathly silence... (*Changing his tone with a smile.*) You talk well, I said to him. But one doesn't say such things without putting up stakes... Shall we agree to a wager? You claim that all women are unfaithful, and that you could seduce anyone's girlfriend in forty-eight hours. I, sir, will give you not forty-eight hours to overcome the virtue of Silvérie, my young mistress, not five days, not ten days, but fifteen days. Do you understand? Fifteen days. Come stay at my hotel. You can find comfortable rooms for as little as three francs... I say that in passing, since I know that you don't mind the expense... Well then, are we agreed? I'll bet you twenty-five louis that you will not attain your goal. And as I said that, I put my hand in my pocket... and found a handkerchief and a pencil stub... But, carried away by the beauty of the gesture, I laid them proudly on the table.

MUCHE: And that period of time expires today?

DODEAU: Today at four o'clock, that is to say, in an hour and a quarter. Oh, don't look at the clock!... It's five and a half hours fast. The former tenant was a young Hindu student who was homesick. He set the clock to the time in Chandernagor, his home town.

MUCHE: And you'll get the money at four o'clock?

DODEAU: If anyone gets it, there's a serious chance that it will be me. I'm so sure of myself that I made no plans for a possible loss, and didn't even go to the Lyon Bank to check my balance.

MUCHE: All the same, it takes a certain nerve to gamble twenty-five louis on a woman's virtue.

DODEAU: You must be joking! Do you know Silvérie?

MUCHE: I knew her before you. She cheated on me with you.

DODEAU: Well, yes... but after a year. We've been together for four months. Now, within the memory of man, Silvérie has never been unfaithful after such a short time. Besides, I know women. And I can tell that she has never been more blindly devoted to me.

MUCHE: That's true.

DODEAU: She's an utterly dependable woman. Adorned with every physical grace, one might say that Nature, ever provident, refused her the gift of intellect only to make her lovelier.

MUCHE: Yes. She is what we might call, in technical terms, a nitwit. If you put something over on her, she accepts it with infinite sweetness. Do you remember when you made her believe, at the train station, that the radiators in first class compartments were filled with kirsch punch...

DODEAU: She is, I repeat, an utterly dependable woman. I should tell you, besides, that I warned her about the bet. That probably wasn't strictly honorable... but since we didn't mention it in the agreement...

MUCHE: How did you tell her? Did you explain it clearly?

DODEAU: I simply said that I had bet twenty-five louis that in fifteen days she wouldn't cheat on me with that Dutchman... I insisted particularly on the twenty-five louis. If she's tempted to forget her duties, she won't forget that amount.

MUCHE: And what did she say?

DODEAU: She was quite struck by it. It left her rather pensive. She said to me, "Oh, my dear, do you really need to win those twenty-five louis?" And I said, "You heard me!"

MUCHE: And you're absolutely sure that nothing has happened?

DODEAU: I'm positive. Silvérie has been preoccupied these past few days, but we haven't brought it up again. Today she went out to the

Louvre. I let her go with joy. The Dutchman hasn't left the hotel. I just learned that he stayed in his room today. But here's Silvérie herself... Here's the beautiful Silvérie!

SCENE III
MUCHE, DODEAU, SILVÉRIE

SILVÉRIE: (*Entering.*) Hello, Muche! (*Kissing Dodeau.*) Victor, I have something to tell you.

MUCHE: I'll leave you, then. Goodbye, Silvérie.

DODEAU: I'll walk out with you, just to check the racing results. The first race at Saint-Ouen must be posted by now. There's a horse I would have liked to bet on, and I'll be annoyed if it won. That's my way of following the races.

SCENE IV
SILVÉRIE, *alone.*

SILVÉRIE: Five minutes to three. One more hour, and the bet would have been lost. Just in time... Don't I love Victor a lot, to have done this? When he told me about it, fifteen days ago, I understood only one thing, that I had to... get to know that Dutchman, so that Victor could win twenty-five louis. I decided to do it, but put it off to the last minute. So, just now, I went to see him, that Dutchman that I detest. I met him several times on the stairs. He provoked me in various ways. But I never answered him. When I opened his door, when I went to him, and said with resignation, "I'm all yours," he seemed absolutely astounded, quite upset... so upset that I was worried, and wondered if he'd have time to get over it before four o'clock. Finally, he regained his composure, and here I am. It was an unpleasant experience, but Victor will be pleased. Here he is.

SCENE V
DODEAU, SILVÉRIE

DODEAU: Here I am, dearest! Well, what did you have to tell me?

SILVÉRIE: Victor, you won!

DODEAU: (*Gently.*) Not yet, dearest! It's only three o'clock. I won't win my bet for another hour.

SILVÉRIE: Did you think I'd wait until the last minute? Victor, you won. It was a difficult moment for me. But you won your five hundred francs. I must love you very much!

DODEAU: (*After looking at her in alarm for a few moments.*) Please explain. There's some confusion in what you say.

SILVÉrie: But it's so simple, my little Victor. I hated that Dutchman, and it cost me a lot to cheat on you. But because I knew that it would bring you twenty-five louis, I bravely played my part. It was only an hour and a half ago. I went to see that man, closed my eyes, and said, "I'm all yours." He took me at my word.

DODEAU: (*He listens, shaking his head mechanically, then finishes by looking at her in terror. He collapses onto the armchair, his head in his hands. Silence. He finally raises his head, and speaks in a frighteningly calm tone.*) The deepest parts of the Atlantic Ocean are approximately two hundred meters. They have been measured in the Gulf of Mexico. The Pacific has produced even more interesting soundings: eight thousand six hundred and six meters, in a trench called the Tuscarora... They gave that name to that part of the Pacific because the English ship that made the soundings was called the *Tuscarora*... (*Looking at Silvérie.*) Well! The sounders of the *Tuscarora*—who are all capable sounders—could all be brought before this delicate little soul. They could play out their longest lines to the end. (*With growing vehemence.*) They could lean over the bulwarks. They could be permitted to hang by their feet from the deck, and to hold the cable with their fingertips. Do you think that they could reach the bottom of this charming soul, of this extraordinary innocence? (*With a smile of triumph.*) They couldn't! (*In a burst.*) You couldn't do it, gentlemen of the *Tuscarora*! (*He flies into a violent rage, and emits frightening cries; then, calming down a bit, says to Silvérie.*) There are no words in our language, or in any European language, sufficient to describe your case. Do you know what I'm reduced to? I'm reduced to crude onomatopoeia, like our ancestors in the caves. You are the lowest of the ha ha ha!... A sorry hoo hoo hoo!... and, to sum it up, a hee hee hee! (*After reflection.*) A hee hee hee! That's the word.

SILVÉRIE: My friend... If I'd known you'd be so angry... I thought I was doing the right thing...

DODEAU: (*In a gentle voice, caressing her cheek.*) No... No... Don't say anything else. (*Indicating his forehead, plaintively.*) This is a human skull, in which there is a human brain. Its resistance is not unlimited. (*He sighs, pulls Silvérie to him, and in a familiar and almost playful tone.*) So then, you don't know what a bet is?

SILVÉRIE: You told me...

DODEAU: If you didn't go see the Dutchman, I won twenty-five louis. If you did go see him, I lost twenty-five louis. Now, instead of it being me, or, if you prefer, rather than it be I who receives five hundred francs, it will be I, Victor, who will be obliged to give them to him.

SILVÉRIE: You'll be obliged?

DODEAU: It's called a debt of honor.

SILVÉRIE: Oh, my darling! I'm terribly unhappy.

DODEAU: (*Controlling himself.*) Don't be. You see that I don't let it upset me... Thunder! (*In an outburst.*) It's nine o'clock in Chandernagor! In a half hour, he'll make his way here, and say in a calm voice, "You have lost."

SILVÉRIE: (*With a doubtful air.*) What do you mean? He's going to come here and say that you lost?

DODEAU: That was our agreement.

SILVÉRIE: And you think he'll say that?... He'll say that?... He'll come here to tell you that I... No, he won't say it! There are gentlemen in Holland.

DODEAU: He'll say it... because it was a bet.

SILVÉRIE: But he mustn't say it... Ah, I've made a terrible blunder. Well, I owe it to myself, I owe it to you, to set things right. I'll go see the Dutchman. He's a gentleman. "Van" is a sign of nobility in Holland. I'll just say a few words to him, and beg him to keep quiet. He'll keep quiet, I assure you. And because you, naturally, will play the part of the man who knows nothing about it, you'll win.

DODEAU: I've listened patiently. I wanted to see if you'd follow this to the end. (*Pointing to himself.*) I have silenced in myself that reserve of inflexible honor that I inherited from centuries of strict education. (*Very calm.*) Well! A curious thing has happened to that reserve of inflexible honor: it has fallen strangely silent. Have I smothered it in spite of myself?... (*Solemnly.*) Go, go, creature of sorrow, go upon your mission of silent devotion. (*Exit Silvérie.*)

SCENE VI
DODEAU, *then* THE BELLBOY

(*Dodeau, after Silvérie exits, falls into a profound silence. Then, with a start, he gravely opens a drawer, takes out a revolver, and lays it heavily on the table. He also takes out a large sheet of white paper, and begins to write. There is a knock at the door.*)

THE BELLBOY: (*Entering.*) The gentleman in room 17 asked me to bring this to you, sir. (*The bellboy exits.*)

DODEAU: (*Opening the letter cautiously, and removing a banknote.*) If I hadn't received this, nothing was left for me but to blow out my brains. (*Returning the revolver to the drawer, in a firm tone.*) And I would have done what I said. (*Approaching his fingers to the banknote, then drawing them back, then touching them to it.*) No burning of the fingers. (*Walking downstage and placing the banknote in his billfold.*) I must tell you that after a fall from a horse, I lost all moral sense.

END

Clara, or A Warm Welcome Richly Rewarded

Lyrical drama in two acts

(The stage shows the central square of a modest village. An old man, leaning painfully on a cane, has just arrived. Children, some mocking, some pitiful, surround and contemplate him.)

THE CHILDREN: (*Moved by a variety of emotions.*)

Where do you go, old man, in these morose Novembers?

Do you seek a retreat where you can rest your members?

The Spanish inn, perhaps? Or Kroumir's place, instead?

THE OLD MAN: (*Very tired, so tired.*)

Can such a wreck as I choose where to lay his head?

Who knows? Now night has come; I seek a sanctuary.

Perhaps I'll find a roof, perhaps a cemetery!

FIRST CHILD: (*Hypocritically.*)

Come to my house, old man; my folks are generous.

(The children gathered here will surely vouch for us.)

We'll make a place for you, and seat you at our table.

SECOND CHILD: (*Angrily, to the first.*)

I think you mean, my friend, a place out in the stable.

Your father is so harsh; your mother cold and vain:

They'd welcome this poor man with malice and disdain.

THIRD CHILD: (*Proudly.*)

Old man, come stay with us. My uncle is a ranger.

You see these peaceful flocks, that graze here safe from danger?

Their shepherds are his charge, and he can level fines.

FOURTH CHILD: (*Well-to-do.*)

My father keeps a bar, and serves the finest wines.

If you go there, I'm sure, before you must continue,

O pallid vagabond, you'll get a bottle in you.

FIFTH CHILD: (*A little girl.*)

The widow of a guard, who draws a pension which

Can barely meet her needs, my mother is not rich.

However, she is young, and really quite a beauty.

THE OLD MAN: (*To the little girl, with enthusiasm.*)

You are a gracious child, and conscious of your duty.

Blonde infant! Lead me there; I'm happy to aver

That I already feel that I'm in love with her.

(The old man, holding the child by the hand, goes off in the direction of the little one's house. Curtain.)

END OF ACT ONE

ACT TWO

(The stage shows the front steps, entwined with ivy, of a country home. As the curtain rises, all three are there, the old man clasping the child's hand with his own left, and his right arm encircling the waist of the young woman, who, for the little girl was not exaggerating, really is quite pretty.)

THE OLD MAN: (*Vehemently.*)

Come gather, village folk, come gather young and old!

The man within your walls, the stranger you behold,

Is not what people think, for gossip can be sordid.

But virtue, in the end, will always be rewarded.

(*Indicating the young woman.*)

I wed this woman now, whose welcome was so kind.

Her mourning now is done; her grief is left behind!

(*He kisses her.*)

The joy that we deserve, my Clara, is upon us!

(*He kisses her again.*)

And may the sun of love shine golden blessings on us!

(*He kisses her yet again; then, as if seized by an inconceivable frenzy, tears off his wig, his false beard, and the rags that he was wearing. He is revealed as a handsome man, sporting a tunic of the finest cut, with the decoration of an Academy officer on his chest, and an administrative sword at this side. He then cries:*)

Whatever your estate, all slanderers repent!

For I'm sub-prefect of this whole arrondissement!

TABLEAU. CURTAIN.

END

The Miserable Wretch and the Good Genie

Fairy tale in one act.

CHARACTERS:
THE MISERABLE WRETCH
THE WAITER
THE GOOD GENIE

(The terrace of a cafe on a somewhat deserted street. Tables, chairs.)

SCENE I

THE WAITER: (*He wipes the tables while vocalizing, as singers do to train their voices, then removes two empty glasses.*) Ah, ah, ah, ah, ah, ah! Hm! Hm! Hm! Hm! It's amazing, I've never felt in such good voice as I do today.

(*He sings.*) O Matilda, idol of my soul!

What an instrument, eh? (*Bitterly.*) And all to serve lousy beer to a bunch of pigs who toss me a few coins as a tip! And this is what we call destiny! Oh, misery!

(*He sings.*) Immortal glory of our ancestors!

How I would triumph tonight at the Grand Opera in Montélimar!... And if I say Montélimar, it's because, in my current position, I can't be too proud!... And yet, with this basso profundo... (*He gestures decisively.*) But enough! If I spew bile, and even more bile, it won't help anything, will it? Well, then...

(*He exits, singing.*) What matter all these treacheries...

SCENE II

THE MISERABLE WRETCH: (*He enters downcast, oh how downcast! and wearing clothes that are clean, but pureed beyond all description. He collapses into a chair.*) Oh, I have my faults, of course, and can't claim to be more perfect than another; but there's one thing that nobody can take away from me, and that is my terrible thirst. Oh, what a thirst! Throughout my long career, fertile in parched conditions of every kind, I do believe that I have never experienced a thirst like this before. (*He takes a ten centime coin from his pocket, and strikes the table with it.*) Waiter!... Nothing makes you thirstier than walking up all those stairs, except maybe walking down them. (*He strikes the table again.*) Waiter!... If I took all the stairs I've gone up and down these past few weeks, and placed them end to end, I'm sure I could have climbed up Mount Olympus. (*He interrupts himself.*) Well, a line of iambic pentameter. (*He declaims with affectation.*) "I'm sure I could have climbed up Mount Olympus." It's not very good iambic pentameter, but it is iambic pentameter. (*He strikes the table again, more loudly.*) Waiter!... If he takes any longer, he'll find nothing but a desiccated corpse.

SCENE III

THE WAITER: All right, all right, I'm hurrying!

THE MISERABLE WRETCH: No offense, but it's none too soon.

THE WAITER: Ah, it's you, my poor fellow! Well, how's it going?

THE MISERABLE WRETCH: Eh!

THE WAITER: Have you found a job at last?

THE MISERABLE WRETCH: Alas, not at all! All the shopkeepers just tell me to check later.

THE WAITER: (*Laughing foolishly.*) Maybe they're looking for a chess player.

THE MISERABLE WRETCH: (*With a shrug.*) You think you're funny, don't you?

THE WAITER: Well, no, but one has to laugh. So, an absinthe, as usual?

THE MISERABLE WRETCH: No, no absinthe yet. I'm too thirsty. Drinking absinthe when you're thirsty, my friend, is an offense to our Creator. Beer will do for that purpose.

THE WAITER: A bock, then?

THE MISERABLE WRETCH: A simple bock.

THE WAITER: Light? Dark?

THE MISERABLE WRETCH: Light! (*Suddenly changing his mind.*) No!... Dark.

THE WAITER: (*Exits singing.*)

Between the brunette and the blonde,

His heart is but a vagabond.

SCENE IV

THE MISERABLE WRETCH: Imbecile! And yet it's true, that song of his. Between blondes and brunettes, my heart has never ceased wandering. There have been blondes for whom I would have refused all the brunettes on earth; and I've known brunettes to whom I would have sacrificed my entire existence. Not to mention certain young ladies with light brown hair, and a few little redheads.

SCENE V

THE WAITER: The requested bock!

THE MISERABLE WRETCH: (*He seizes the mug and empties it in one gulp, much to the waiter's amazement.*) This beer is not drinkable.

THE WAITER: (*Contemplating the empty mug.*) And if it were?

THE MISERABLE WRETCH: I'd order another.

THE WAITER: (*Lightly.*) Oh well, beer isn't really our specialty here.

THE MISERABLE WRETCH: So I noticed.

THE WAITER: (*Changing the subject.*) And you, my poor man, still pounding the pavement?

THE MISERABLE WRETCH: Yes, alas! And my savings are starting to run out. (*He counts his money.*) I have one franc and forty centimes to see me through the year.

THE WAITER: That's not much.

THE MISERABLE WRETCH: One franc and forty centimes! A reserve fund which, although apparently sufficient for certain financial associations that I would prefer not to designate more clearly, is rather meager for one man!... But enough! Let us hope! Let us forget! And now, bring me an absinthe, my friend! Absinthe is oblivion! Absinthe is the celestial escape from this terrestrial prison that we call life.

THE WAITER: (*Musingly.*) That may be true.

THE MISERABLE WRETCH: Now and then, you see a man in the gutter. You say, "He's drunk." No! He's just escaped.

THE WAITER: And the police clap him in jail to teach him to escape some other time. Do you want your absinthe straight?

THE MISERABLE WRETCH: No, with anisette.

THE WAITER (*Exits singing.*)

My children, I'm the anisette,

The anisette of Cusenier.

SCENE VI

THE MISERABLE WRETCH: That man's cheerfulness is positively indecent! It just reminds me that he has a job, and I don't. And what a charming occupation! A bringer of oblivion!

SCENE VII

THE WAITER: (*Enters singing.*)

Now has come the sacred hour

When the absinthe is in flower.

THE MISERABLE WRETCH: Cheerful, aren't you, my friend?

THE WAITER: Me? Oh, good heavens, I'm not cheerful.

THE MISERABLE WRETCH: But you sing all the time.

THE WAITER: A man is not cheerful just because he sings.

THE MISERABLE WRETCH: And yet...

THE WAITER: No, the truth is that I sing because I'm a singer.

THE MISERABLE WRETCH: A singer?

THE WAITER: Certainly... Do I look like a mere waiter in a cafe, like all the others? Why no, not at all! (*Drawing himself up.*) I am a lyric artist.

THE MISERABLE WRECH: A strange combination!

THE WAITER: Ah, my dear sir, it's an even stranger story, and... Do you have a minute?

THE MISERABLE WRETCH: Do I have a minute? I have a hundred, a thousand minutes! I have nothing else! Tell me your story, my friend.

THE WAITER: Very well, and you'll see that you're not the only unhappy man on earth.

THE MISERABLE WRETCH: Society is poorly organized.

THE WAITER: Well, just imagine, a few years ago I made my debut as a waiter in a little restaurant, near the Opéra-Comique... you know, the old one.

THE MISERABLE WRETCH: Yes, the one that already burned down.

THE WAITER: Yes... Well, one fine day, here come some gentlemen, proper gentlemen, journalists, who discover that I have a superb voice, and I mean a superb voice! Everyone predicts that I'll end up in the opera. I waste no time; I take voice lessons, and, before long, make my debut in a little theater in the country.

THE MISERABLE WRETCH: Congratulations!

THE WAITER: Ah, yes! And yet no sooner did I debut than I lost my voice. (*He points to his throat, and imitates a mute*.) No more voice than your hand! Oh, it was a lot of fun!... So then, I went back to my waiter's apron.

THE MISERABLE WRETCH: It's a profession as good as any other.

THE WAITER: I don't agree. But let me continue. After only a week of serving beer and cordials, my voice returned! Quite a surprise, eh?

THE MISERABLE WRETCH: (*Coldly*.) Nothing surprises me.

THE WAITER: When I see that my instrument is back, what do I do? I toss away my apron, and book another engagement.

THE MISERABLE WRETCH: And then?

THE WAITER: (*Sadly*.) Oh, you can guess the rest.

THE MISERABLE WRETCH: You lost your voice again?

THE WAITER: Exactly! And from that moment on, it was always the same: a magnificent voice when I was a waiter, and nothing when I had to sing *William Tell*.

THE MISERABLE WRETCH: The situation is not without a certain piquancy! Do you know what you should do?

THE WAITER: Tell me.

THE MISERABLE WRETCH: Try to get a job in a cabaret. You could sing your repertory while you serve refreshments.

THE WAITER: There's an idea. I'll give it some thought.

THE MISERABLE WRETCH: Alas! I don't have that option myself. I am neither a singer, nor a waiter, but only an accountant, an unemployed accountant, due to lack of work.

THE WAITER: Don't despair, my friend. I'm sure that you'll find a good job, just when you least expect it.

THE MISERABLE WRETCH: I'll accept your prediction, since my

patience is at an end. All that walking, all that humiliation!

THE WAITER: (*Grave.*) Humiliation! I know it well.

THE MISERABLE WRETCH: (*Philosophical.*) Oh, humiliation, to be honest, is the least of my worries. For some time now, I've put on a face that is beyond blushes.

THE WAITER: (*Ironic.*) So your hat blushes for you.

THE MISERABLE WRETCH: (*Removing his hat and observing that it has, indeed, turned red.*) The fact is that my old topper is becoming quite scarlet.

THE WAITER: On the other hand, your coat is turning a lovely shade of green.

THE MISERABLE WRETCH: There you have the mysteries of Nature! Who can explain why Time, that strange colorist, amuses himself by making old hats red, while he tints antique black frock coats green. (*He holds his hat to the sleeve of his coat.*) The green of my coat sets off the red of my hat quite wonderfully.

THE WAITER: And vice versa.

THE MISERABLE WRETCH: Brought together in this way, my coat seems greener, and my hat redder.

THE WAITER: Which is not so bad, come to think of it.

THE MISERABLE WRETCH: Nevertheless, I would prefer a less polychromatic outfit... When will I be able to afford a new suit from La Belle Jardinière?

THE WAITER: That's none too ambitious on your part.

THE MISERABLE WRETCH: I've never been ambitious. With a hundred sous a day, I could have been the happiest of men.

THE WAITER: A hundred sous a day! I must say, that's not the wealth of the Incas.

THE MISERABLE WRETCH: I would be thoroughly satisfied with it, myself. But where's the good genie who could assure me a hundred sous a day?

(Celestial music is heard, suddenly interrupting the two men's conversation.)

SCENE VIII

THE GOOD GENIE: A good genie! Who mentioned a good genie? Present and accounted for!

(The miserable wretch and the waiter fall in ecstasy and join hands.)

THE MISERABLE WRETCH: What?... You're...

THE GOOD GENIE: Yes, a good genie... What's amazing about that?

THE MISERABLE WRETCH: Oh, nothing... Or, well, yes! It's not a common occurrence!

THE GOOD GENIE: Are you the one who called me, miserable wretch?

THE MISERABLE WRETCH: I'm the one.

THE GOOD GENIE: You did well, miserable wretch, for I am never invoked in vain. What can I do for you?

THE MISERABLE WRETCH: I was just saying to this gentleman that I've never been ambitious.

THE GOOD GENIE: So, a hundred sous a day would be enough for you?

THE MISERABLE WRETCH: More than enough.

THE GOOD GENIE: Well, then! Be happy, miserable wretch. Your wish will be granted.

THE MISERABLE WRETCH: *(Ecstatic.)* Really? You can do that for me?

THE GOOD GENIE: Why yes, you little fool. Nothing could be simpler... Only, because I have other things to do than bring you a... What do you call it, simple mortals?

THE WAITER: A fiver.

THE GOOD GENI: That's it, a fiver! Because I have other things to do than bring you a fiver every morning, I'll give it to you in one lump sum.

THE MISERABLE WRETCH: (*Not believing his ears.*) In one lump sum!... The whole amount in one lump sum! (*He gestures, as if piling heaps of gold on the table.*) One lump sum!

THE WAITER: (*In wonder, repeating the gesture.*) One lump sum! Aren't you the lucky one! I was just saying that things would turn out well for you.

THE MISERABLE WRETCH: (*To the good genie.*) And... when can you give me this little windfall?

THE GOOD GENIE: You're impatient, miserable wretch! I need a little time to figure out the amount. Wait here a minute. I'll be right back. (*He leaves to the sound of celestial music.*)

SCENE IX

THE WAITER: Well! You can certainly boast about your good luck now! You were looking for a job, and what do you find? A fortune!

THE MISERABLE WRETCH: (*With a grimace.*) Oh, some fortune! A hundred sous a day!

THE WAITER: You were stupid not to ask for more.

THE MISERABLE WRETCH: How was I to know?

THE WAITER: What will you do with all the money?

THE MISERABLE WRETCH: I'll start by buying a hat that isn't so red and a coat that isn't so green. That would be a change.

THE WAITER: If I were you, I'd buy a green hat and a red coat. That would be even more of a change.

THE MISERABLE WRETCH: I'll do nothing of the kind. A true gentleman must, above all, avoid garish colors in his wardrobe.

THE WAITER: You'll have quite a party, I suppose?

THE MISERABLE WRETCH: (*With a shrug.*) A party! The high life! Hey hey! A sugar daddy for chorus girls! All that on a hundred sous a day! You're mad, my friend.

THE WAITER: There are chorus girls, and then there are chorus girls. Come to think of it, I know one myself, at the Moulin de la Galette.

THE MISERABLE WRETCH: (*Pensive.*) It's true, I was stupid... I should have asked for a louis. It wouldn't cost that genie anything!

THE WAITER: (*Struck with a sudden idea.*) I just thought of something. Since you're getting all your loot in one lump sum (*He makes the gesture of heaping up gold.*), what's to stop you from investing it, rather than living on the capital?

THE MISERABLE WRETCH: I don't know if that would be honest. I have the right to a hundred sous a day, not six francs.

THE WAITER: Your scruples do you honor; but if I were you, I'd keep them to myself.

THE MISERABLE WRETCH: (*Hesitant.*) I'll think about it.

THE WAITER: Or even better, buy a cabaret. That's the way to make money!

THE MISERABLE WRETCH: I see what you're getting at. A cabaret where you could warble your ballads while serving brandied cherries.

THE WAITER: (*Singing.*) When shall we be in cherry time...

THE MISERABLE WRETCH: (*Interrupting him with a gesture.*) Shush! (*Celestial music.*) My celestial benefactor returns. (*Worried.*) But where did he put all my money? He doesn't look bent under the weight of it.

THE WAITER: Maybe he's bringing it in banknotes.

THE MISERABLE WRETCH: Or in checks.

SCENE X

THE GOOD GENIE: Hello again, miserable wretch! I hope you weren't too bored in my absence.

THE MISERABLE WRETCH: Not at all, I was chatting with this gentleman. I was planning my future.

THE GOOD GENIE: Ah!

THE MISERABLE WRETCH: Why, yes... I still haven't decided.

THE GOOD GENIE: You will in a minute. (*He places in his hand seven francs and fifty centimes.*) There, miserable wretch!

THE MISERABLE WRETCH: (*Contemplating his seven and a half francs with bewilderment.*) What? What's this?

THE GOOD GENIE: It's your money.

THE MISERABLE WRETCH: My money?... Seven and a half francs? But you told me I'd get it in one lump sum!

THE GOOD GENIE: The amount that I have given you, miserable wretch, represents your full payment.

THE MISERABLE WRETCH: (*Refusing to understand.*) Seven and a half francs? No, no, you're joking. That's all that's coming to me? Tell me that you're joking.

THE GOOD GENIE: I'm afraid, miserable wretch, that good genies never joke.

THE MISERABLE WRETCH: Seven and a half francs!... But then, if I can count—and I can indeed count, because I'm a professional accountant—I have only a day and half to live?

THE GOOD GENIE: Alas, miserable wretch! My powers do not permit me to prolong your existence. I'm sorry.

THE MISERABLE WRETCH: And what about me? Still a day and a half to live!

THE GOOD GENIE: Exactly thirty-six hours.

THE WAITER: That's not much.

THE GOOD GENIE: Try to accept your fate, miserable wretch.

THE MISERABLE WRETCH: My fate? But it's all figured out! (*Cheerfully warming to the subject.*) Oh la la, I've seen worse! (*He tosses his hat in the air and throws his leg on the table.*) Let's go then, I'm no grandpa! My motto from now on is "short but lively!" I'm off to the chorus girls at the Moulin de la Galette! And to start things off: waiter, a Pernod!

THE WAITER: With anisette?

THE MISERABLE WRETCH: No, straight.

THE WAITER: Straight Pernod. (*He sings to the air from Faust.*)

Straight Pernod, Pernod so bright,

Take him up into the light.

Fly him up from all of this,

Up into eternal bliss.

ALL: (*Sing.*)

Straight Pernod, Pernod so bright,

Take him up into the light.

APOTHEOSIS. CURTAIN.

The English Accent

A monologue to be recited at the annual party for the Society of Patient Listeners

Ladies and gentlemen:

Please allow me, before I begin, to beg your indulgence, your complete indulgence.

I will need it, for I, who stand before you, am in no way a professional artist.

An amateur, a simple amateur, is all that I am.

The only merit that I possess, if I do indeed possess any merit, is that I offer you a completely new act. And heavens! In these days of servile imitation in which we now wallow, a new act doesn't grow on trees, eh?

A new act! Admit that you're intrigued. You say to yourself: what on earth can this gentleman do that has never been done before?

You rack your brains, you entertain a thousand suppositions, each more fantastic than the last.

And yet you haven't guessed it; and however clever and astute you may be, ladies and gentlemen, you cannot imagine the nature of the curious exercise that I will soon undertake before you.

I am neither a musician, a prestidigitator, nor an acrobat. I do not even perform monologues (I don't know if you're like me, but I have a horror of monologues).

A poet? No, I am not a poet. I am none of the above, no, I... (*He approaches the audience, and gives enormous importance to his declaration.*)

I imitate an English accent. (*He seems quite astonished at the audience's reaction to this little announcement.*)

I perceive upon the lips, otherwise quite ravishing, of some women present a trace of a mocking smile.

Upon the masculine features of the gentlemen, obvious disappointment is clearly portrayed.

You say to yourself: here is a gentleman who has the pretension to announce something new, and merely intends to imitate an English accent. How lovely, his novelty! How fresh, his innovation! (*Mockingly imitating an English accent.*) Plum pudding! All right! My trousers! My shirt! My wife! Aoh yes! Very well!

(*Resuming his normal accent.*) Let me assure you, ladies and gentlemen: no, it is not this ignoble vaudeville Englishman whom I shall have the honor to imitate before you. The Englishman whom I shall have the honor, I repeat, to imitate before you, is, on the contrary, a fashionable Englishman, well bred, and of high intellectual attainment, one of those Englishmen, more numerous than you may think, who is quite up to date on our language and literature.

First of all, my Englishman was born in France.

Why do you smile? What is so astonishing about an Englishman born in France?

No day passes, no night goes by, without an English baby coming into the world in France.

Just as a French infant could perfectly well be born in London, or in Liverpool.

Thus, my Englishman, and I insist upon this point, which is of some importance, was born in France, and—I go even further—born of a French mother.

Again, I see smiles that I cannot explain... and I continue.

To underline the difference that separates my Englishman from the vulgar plum pudding of the cabaret, I go even further.

Not only was this gentleman born in France, of a French mother, but, what is more, his father was also French.

That, I believe, is a situation well and clearly stated: we have an Englishman, born in France, of French parents.

Since, after the baby's birth, his parents never returned to England—where, besides, they had never set foot—our young islander (if, under such circumstances, we can confer that quality upon him) was raised in France, and in French.

At the Condorcet school, where he received his education, given the choice of German or English for his language requirement, he chose German; so that he never learned a word of English.

.....

At this point, a veritable hailstorm of baked potatoes darkened the firmament.

Our amiable speaker thought it best to retire without further insistence.

The Polisher, or Patience and the Passage of Time Do More than Force or Rage

CHARACTERS:

RAPHAEL CIMAISE, *painter, 23 years old, minus a few weeks (Rage).*

COLIN-CRAMPON, *salesman, 59 years, 11 months, and 29 days old (Patience and the passage of time).*

AN OFFICER OF THE PEACE, *of indeterminate age (Force).*

(The studio of a painter in Montmartre. Sketches, plasters, a framed painting on an easel, an old chest, etc., etc., a mannequin draped with old fabric. Almost everywhere, flowers in vases.)

SCENE I

RAPHAEL CIMAISE: (*He arranges the flowers and drapery, standing back at times to judge the result.*) There!... That's not too bad now, I think. And besides, what I like about my little arrangement is that it doesn't look too prepared. When the Countess arrives, momentarily, I think her first impression will be a good one. Let's see the effect when you come in. (*He exits, closing the door, then returns immediately, looking around and smiling with a satisfied air, then, imitating a woman's voice.*) But your place is charming, my dear artist, utterly charming! (*Resuming his normal voice.*) I don't think I put out enough corylopsis. It still smells too much like my pipe. (*He takes a vaporizer and sprays scent around himself.*) And I almost forgot! Ah! Thank you very much! (*He seizes the pipe rack and sniffs it.*) Ah! Phew! Where can I put this? There, in the chest. Well, that's nice, Irma broke! Such a good pipe, and so well seasoned! (*He sprays heavily where the pipe rack had been.*) These fine ladies are so delicate! One detail, one little nothing, can offend them. And she is a fine lady. (*Addressing the mannequin.*) Surprised, aren't you, old girl? A fine lady, a genuine countess! Maybe I should spray a little on myself. (*He sprays himself, and sniffs the air.*) That's beginning to do some good. Hmm, maybe I used too much now. Well, better too much than too little. (*He looks at the clock.*) Five to five. Another five minutes, and she'll be here. And she will be here, she promised. (*Imitating a woman's voice.*) So be it, my dear artist. (*Resuming his normal voice.*) She always calls me her dear artist. (*Imitating a woman's voice again.*) I shall visit your studio at five o'clock. (*Normal voice.*) Then she added with a bizarre expression, and in a tone of voice that stood my hair on end, "But with completely honorable intentions, of course." They always say that. (*He glances automatically at the divan, scratches his head, and rearranges the cushions.*) With completely honorable intentions! And she looked at me so insistently... I don't know, but I suspect that we won't be too bored here in about fifteen minutes. Well, she's a fine lady, let's say thirty minutes. A car! Here she is! (*He rushes to the window.*) No, it didn't stop. This is stupid, I'm so nervous. Another car... It's stopping! Here she is! Damn it, it's some fat man. (*Looking at the clock.*) And besides, it's not five o'clock yet, anyway. One minute can seem so long; I never would have believed it. (*There is a knock at the door.*) And suddenly, here she is! (*Quickly he turns up his mustache, pulls and smooths a lock of hair over his forehead, and assumes his most gracious smile, while crumpling his Lavallière cravat.*) Come in!

SCENE II

(Raphael stands stupefied at the sight of the visitor who now presents himself.)

RAPHAEL: (*Brusquely.*) You have the wrong place, sir, you made a mistake. (*Colin-Crampon gestures that he is too winded to speak, but that this is indeed where he wanted to come, and wipes his forehead.*) Let me repeat, sir, you made a mistake, this is the wrong place. I'm not expecting anyone. (*Aside.*) And the Countess due any minute! (*He tries to take the man by the arm and show him out.*)

COLIN-CRAMPON: I'm sorry, sir, but six flights is a bit of a climb. I'm no longer young. Only fifteen years ago, sir, I could have swallowed your six flights in one mouthful.

RAPHAEL: But sir...

COLIN-CRAMPON: My word, you're lively when you're twenty, but you'll see when you're my age. I'm short of breath.

RAPHAEL: You may be short of breath, but I'm short of time.

COLIN-CRAMPON: Ah, you're short of time! Well, I won't keep you long, for I know what it is to be short of time. Sir, I have sought you out in order to offer you a great service.

RAPHAEL: A service! What service? And make it quick, because I'm expecting someone.

COLIN-CRAMPON: Huh! You just said you weren't expecting anyone.

RAPHAEL: I was mistaken. I'm expecting someone on urgent business, and...

COLIN-CRAMPON: Urgent business! Well, then, I'll cut my visit short. I know about business. Business is business, as those diabolical Americans say. You should never put off for tomorrow what you can do the day after. That's my principle.

RAPHAEL: Sir, if you will just explain...

COLIN-CRAMPON: (*Examining the studio.*) You have a nice place here. (*Sniffing the air.*) And it smells really good. But good lord! A lot of your things do need polishing!

RAPHAEL: Sir!...

COLIN-CRAMPON: Oh, there's no need to take offense at that. One can be quite clean, and still have poorly polished furnishings.

RAPHAEL: Sir, could you get to the point? I have no time to lose.

COLIN-CRAMPON: Very well put. No time to lose. Lost time is never regained. I know all about that. I've worked all my life, sir. I'm fifty-nine years old, with three children, including one married daughter. And she married well, too. But say, you must know my son-in-law, Labrousse, one of your colleagues. He paints automobiles.

RAPHAEL: No, I don't know your Labrosse.

COLIN-CRAMPON: Excuse me, not Labrosse, Labrousse.

RAPHAEL: I don't care! Will you please leave!

COLIN-CRAMPON: True, I do ramble on, and I believe you're pressed for time.

RAPHAEL: Get out of here! (*Aside.*) A car is stopping! It's her, I'm sure. (*He runs to the window.*) No.

COLIN-CRAMPON: Aha, you rascal, you're expecting a woman. Ah, I was like that myself in my day. When you're waiting for your lovely, waiting can be cruel.

RAPHAEL: Oh, the brute, the brute!

COLIN-CRAMPON: Let's get back to the subject. (*He takes a bottle from his pocket.*) Do you see this little bottle?

RAPHAEL: What is it?

COLIN-CRAMPON: What is it, you ask? A marvel, sir, simply a marvel. (*With the volubility of a barker.*) This is the fruit of twenty years of ceaseless toil. This little bottle is Brilliant, otherwise known as Brilliant Sun. There is nothing like a brilliant sun, as the song says. With this product, sir, you not only make things brilliant, but shimmering, shining, scintillating, sparkling, resplendent, flamboyant, dazzling, blinding, stupefying! With this liquid, sir, (*indicating various objects as he continues*) no more dull woodwork, rusted iron, tarnished copper, greasy crystal, soiled picture frames! With my product, my good man, everything is shimmering, everything is sparkling, everything is resplendent, everything is flamboyant, everything is dazzling, everything is blinding.

RAPHAEL: (*Thoroughly discouraged.*) You already said that.

COLIN-CRAMPON: Don't interrupt, sir. My product can be applied to all materials, known or unknown: wood, leather, marble, porcelain, pottery, plaster, terra cotta, iron, copper, silver, gold, celluloid, varnish, linoleum, oilcloth, paintings, sculptures, castings, and even shoes. My product, sir, is as indispensable to the artist as it is to the worker, to the crowned head as it is to the simple farmer. It has its place in sumptuous palaces as well as in humble cottages, in the mansion as well as in the studio. The President of our Republic himself is not too proud to use it to give his ceremonial decorations that incomparable luster that is the envy of foreign courts. And you, sir, cannot do without my product for your pictures, for your frames, for everything! A piece of flannel, folded over, a few drops of my liquid, just like that, and you rub lightly. (*He rubs a picture frame.*)

RAPHAEL: (*Aside.*) The man is insane. What will the Countess say if she finds this lunatic here?

COLIN-CRAMPON: Wait, sir, take a look and judge! Look at the result! Did I exaggerate? And on wood, too! Take a look. (*He rubs the chest.*)

RAPHAEL: (*In a rage.*) I am no longer responsible for my actions! Get out!

COLIN-CRAMPON: And the same result on leather. (*He puts his foot on the chest and rubs his shoe.*) Is that dazzling enough for you? And tough! You can rub it with your finger. (*He takes Raphael's hand and forces him to rub the shoe*.) No, rub hard, don't be scared. Now wet your finger and rub away; my polish still holds. What do you say to that, eh?

RAPHAEL: I say that I've had enough of this! Do you see the door?

COLIN-CRAMPON: Perfect, the door! The same result! You'll see! (*He starts to rub the doorknob*.)

RAPHAEL: This is too much! I can't deal with this old man. I'm calling the police. (*He goes to the window*.) There's an officer now! Psst! Psst! Officer, could you please come up here?

COLIN-CRAMPON: Take a look. Prejudice aside, it's beautiful, I tell you! With a single bottle of my product, in one year you can polish one hundred and fifty doorknobs, three tables, twelve chairs, ten picture frames, and twenty pairs of shoes, and all for the truly ridiculous price of... no, you'll laugh, of three francs and sixty-five centimes. Wasn't I right to say it was stupefying? How many bottles shall I put you down for? (*There is a knock*.)

RAPHAEL: Come in!

SCENE III

THE OFFICER: Did someone here call me?

RAPHAEL: Yes, I did.

THE OFFICER: What's the matter?

RAPHAEL: The matter is that I ask you to remove this man immediately.

THE OFFICER: Aha! And what has this man done?

RAPHAEL: He's been polishing my furniture for the last fifteen minutes.

THE OFFICER: Aha! I see. And you don't want to pay him.

COLIN-CRAMPON: But I'm not asking for anything.

RAPHAEL: This is all I need!

THE OFFICER: (*To Raphael.*) What's this? A man polishes your furniture for free, and you call on armed force to remove him. This is all very unclear. (*Taking out his notepad.*) First of all, your first and last name?

RAPHAEL: My first and last name have nothing to do with this.

THE OFFICER: Ah, that's what you think! You suppose that a simple citizen can disturb an officer of the peace without providing his civil status. Do you even have a civil status? And besides, (*examining the studio*) where are we?

RAPHAEL: We are in my place.

THE OFFICER: We'll have to tell d'Ache about this. (*He sniffs the air.*) This is some prostitute's room.

RAPHAEL: A prostitute?

THE OFFICER: Obviously a prostitute. All those flowers, that perfume. I've seen it all before; this is a prostitute's room. And you refuse to give me your first and last name?

RAPHAEL: My name is Raphael Cimaise, and I request that you eject this man immediately.

THE OFFICER: Not so fast! I may just eject you first.

RAPHAEL: Oh, this is too much!

THE OFFICER: There's no "this is too much" about it. Try to explain yourself properly. What objection do you have to this man? (*Addressing Colin-Crampon.*) Or rather, sir, tell me what this little fop has against you. You look smarter than him.

COLIN-CRAMPON: I can explain everything, sergeant. (*The officer is visibly flattered.*)

RAPHAEL: But, sir...

THE OFFICER: Keep quiet, you!

COLIN-CRAMPON: I'm particularly pleased that I have the chance to offer you a great service.

THE OFFICER: Who, me?

COLIN-CRAMPON: Yes, you, absolutely. (*He examines him from head to toe.*) Tell me, my good man, what do you use to polish your shoes?

THE OFFICER: (*Baffled.*) I beg your pardon?

COLIN-CRAMPON: What do you use to polish your shoes?

THE OFFICER: (*Laughing.*) Shoe polish, I suppose.

COLIN-CRAMPON: Shoe polish! You're all the same! Well, my friend, in the future don't use shoe polish. Even the best is worthless. Shoe polish is death to shoes. It burns the leather, it disintegrates it, it rots it. Yes, sergeant, it rots it.

THE OFFICER: That's entirely possible.

COLIN-CRAMPON: Whereas with a simple piece of flannel and a few drops of my product, like this... May I? (*He takes the officer's foot, places it on the chest, and starts polishing the shoe.*) Instantly, you obtain a brilliant shine. See for yourself! Isn't it beautiful?

THE OFFICER: (*Admiring his shoe.*) The truth is that it's wonderful!

COLIN-CRAMPON: With the same piece of flannel, you add more of my product, and get the same result with your belt buckle. (*He polishes the belt buckle, as the officer gazes in delight.*)

THE OFFICER: All I can say is that it's wonderful! It's too bad you don't have a button board, you could polish my buttons.

COLIN-CRAMPON: A button board? No, I don't have one on me. (*To Raphael.*) Tell me, young man, would you happen to have a button board?

RAPHAEL: (*Exploding.*) That does it! A button board! Yes, I'm bored with you butting in here! I've had enough! My patience is at an end! (*He seizes the fire tongs and brandishes them.*) A button board! He asks if I have a button board! Get out! Get out, both of you, or I'll attack you! Out with you! (*He collars both of them, pushes them outside, and locks the door.*) I can't breathe! A car! (*He rushes to the window.*) It's her! It's the Countess! (*He opens the door and finds himself face to face with the officer and Colin-Crampon, who throw themselves upon him, and pin his arms.*)

THE OFFICER: Aha, my fine fellow, we have you now! Your case is clear. Assaulting an officer during the exercise of his duties.

COLIN-CRAMPON: Ambush.

THE OFFICER: Death threats.

COLIN-CRAMPON: (*Indicating the tongs.*) With a firearm.

THE OFFICER: You can count on at least ten years. Come on, to the station!

RAPHAEL: Oh, my God! And the Countess is on the stairs!

END

Translator's Notes

Coquelin Cadet was first published in *Le Chat Noir,* November 17, 1888. As mentioned in the introduction, Allais wrote it under the name of Francisque Sarcey.

Paul Bourget was a novelist and journalist, a defender of religion against science.

Paul Ollendorff published many short plays and monologues by Coquelin, Allais, Cros, and others.

Jules Lévy was a member of the Hydropathes, and founded the Arts Incohérents; he mostly published works by his friends.

Léon Gandillot was best known as a playwright (his play *The Turtle* contained an undressing scene that scandalized New York audiences). He took over as editor of *Le Chat Noir* when Allais left.

General Boulanger was a populist politician, Charles Chincholle a journalist who supported him. In the original, a slice of bread says "mince" ("thin," but also a euphemism for "merde"). Although the other jokes do come from Coquelin's *Pirouettes,* this one does not. Yes, I did check.

A Poor Man (*L'homme pauvre*) was first published in *L'Hydropathe,* February 19, 1879.

My Pal Mittick (*Mon ami Lôz*) was inscribed in the *Livre d'Or du Chat Noir,* a sort of guestbook, around 1882. The original title was a pun on "amylose," in keeping with Allais's reputation as a pharmacist; I've substituted a pun on "palmitic."

It was clearly inspired by Charles Cros's monologue, *Le hareng saur,* as mentioned in the introduction.

The Calf (*Le Veau*), was first published in *Le Chat Noir,* December 20, 1884, and reprinted in Allais's first collection, *À se tordre* (*Double Over*) in 1891. Sara was the daughter of Rodolphe Salis, the proprietor of Le Chat Noir.

As Good a Way as Any (*Un moyen comme un autre*) was published in *Le Chat Noir,* February 28, 1885, and reprinted in *À se tordre.* Guy-Charles was the son of Charles Cros, and later a poet himself.

The Miserable Wretch and the Good Genie (*Le pauvre bougre et le bon génie*) was first published as a story in *Le Chat Noir,* August 1, 1885; printed as a monologue in 1890 by Ollendorff; then collected in Allais's 1893 collection *Pas de Bile!* (*No Bile!*). The subtitle is found only in the Ollendorff. Allais later expanded it into a one-act (see below.)

The late Scribe was the prolific playwright and librettist Eugène Scribe, who, in fact, probably did not write that line.

The Gnu (*Le gnou*) appeared in *Le Chat Noir,* December 12, 1885. There is, of course, no Brazilian legend about the gnu, which is native to Africa.

An Invention (*Une invention*) appeared in *Le Chat Noir,* June 12, 1886, and was reprinted in *À se tordre.* In the *Almanach illustré du Père Ubu* (Alfred Jarry, 1901), Ubu also invents the umbrella after being caught in the rain on the rue de Rivoli. Homage? Plagiarism? Coincidence?

A White Night for a Red Hussar (*La nuit blanche d'un hussard rouge*) first appeared in *Le Chat Noir*, January 8, 1887, and was published later that year by Ollendorff. It was reprinted in *Pas de Bile!*

A Luminous Idea (*Une idée lumineuse*) first appeared in *Le Chat Noir*, November 19, 1887, as *Un Inventeur*. It was published as a monologue, under its new title, by Ollendorff in 1888, and then reprinted in *Pas de Bile!* The subtitle is found only in the Ollendorff edition.

The Doctor (*Le médecin*) first appeared in *Le Chat Noir*, December 15, 1888, and was reprinted in *À se tordre*.

A Malcontent (*Un mécontent*) first appeared in *Le Chat Noir*, February 23, 1889, was published as a chapbook by Ollendorff that year, and then reprised in Allais's 1892 collection, *Vive la Vie!* The subtitle was added to the Ollendorff edition. When it was reprinted in *Vive la Vie!*, Allais added a note: "I have insisted on publishing this story, despite its rather stale topicality, to show future generations the attitude of certain French citizens in the years of our grace 1889-1891." As mentioned in a previous note, General Boulanger was a populist politician, especially active in those years.

Untitled (*Sans titre*) appeared in *Le Journal*, November 19, 1892. Allais later used the imaginary revue title, *We Are Not Cattle*, for his 1896 collection.

At the Publisher (*Chez l'éditeur*) appeared in *Le Chat Noir*, April 8, 1893.

Eight Days Later (*Huit jours après*) appeared in *Le Journal*,

August 7, 1893. Allais had published an earlier, shorter version in *Le Chat Noir,* July 14, 1883.

Gum syrup, sugar syrup thickened with gum arabic, was more popular then than now.

Magnum's Revenge (*La vengeance de Magnum*) debuted in *Le Journal*, May 15, 1894, and reappeared in the 1895 collection *2 + 2 = 5.*

La Nouvelle Cirque, founded by Joseph Oller in 1886, offered pantomimes, clowns, acrobats, riders, and water ballet; it was noted especially for its large indoor pool. It operated until 1926.

Tonton in Society (*Tonton dans le monde*) was published in *Le Journal*, November 29, 1895, and reprinted in Allais's 1896 collection, *On n'est pas des boeufs* (*We Are Not Cattle*).

The Playwright and the Director, or One Year Later (*L'auteur dramatique et le directeur de théâtre, ou un an après*) appeared in *Le Journal*, March 10, 1896.

Official Rehabilitation (*Réhabilitation solennelle*) appeared in *Le Journal*, October 27, 1896. That year, Allais and Alfred Capus wrote the play *Innocent*, also about a miscarriage of justice.

A Scrupulous Woman (*Une femme scrupuleuse*) was published in *Le Journal*, October 31, 1896. "And isn't that better than going to the cafe?" was one of Allais's catchphrases, usually invoked, as here, in mock morality.

Silvérie, or The Dutch Fund (*Silvérie, ou les fonds hollandais*) was written with Tristan Bernard, and first performed May 19, 1898, at the Théâtre des Capucines. It was based on Allais's story *Simple malentendu* (*Simple Misunderstanding*), first published in *Le Chat Noir*, March 29, 1890, and collected in *À se tordre*. In the story, Dodeau is the narrator, Silvérie is Angéline, there is no Muche, and Van Heitner is Van Deyck-Lister. The original version was dedicated to Coquelin Cadet, so perhaps Allais thought it might work as a monologue as well. This adaptation, it must be said, probably owes more to Bernard than to Allais. The name Van Heitner may have been inspired by Major Heitner, a friend of both Allais and Bernard; Heitner later appeared in several films directed by Raymond Bernard, Tristan's son.

Silvérie later formed the basis for the novel *Le Boomerang, ou Rien n'est mal qui finit bien* (*The Boomerang, or Nothing is Bad That Ends Well*), serialized under Allais's name in *Le Journal* in 1903, but ghostwritten by, as Allais put it, "a young confectioner." In *Le Boomerang*, Dodeau, Muche, Silvérie, and Van Heitner become Népomucène Le Briquetier, Guillaume de la Renforcerie, Marie-Blanche Loison, and Berg-op-Zoom. The novelization is accomplished by outrageous padding; to add further verbiage, Marie-Blanche plays the Good Genie in a performance of *The Miserable Wretch and The Good Genie,* which is transcribed line for line, with additional footnotes, audience reactions, and other stuffing.

With an unexplained respelling (*Sylvérie*), the play resurfaced as a TV movie in 1965, directed by Michel Ayats. The cast included Jacques Toja (Dodeau), Armand Meffre (Muche, here changed to Munsche), Bernadette Laffont (Sylvérie), and André Andrès (the bellboy).

Clara, or a Warm Welcome Richly Rewarded (*Clara, ou le bon acceuil princièrement recompensé*) was first published in *Le Journal,* October 30, 1898, and reprinted in Allais's 1899 collection, *Pour cause du fin du bail* (*Because the Rent Is Due*).

In a subsequent column, on November 20, Allais informed his readers that Clara would be the subject of a musical competition: "Composers such as Théodore Dubois and Pugno (in collaboration), Debussy, Charpentier, Léopold Dauphin, Erik Satie, and others of equal stature have not hesitated to take part in this contest. Therefore, *Clara, or a Warm Welcome Richly Rewarded* will soon be performed in the Journal's Festival Hall. But, it was objected in high places, won't it be a little monotonous, the same play performed several times in a row, monotonous even with different scores? The observation seemed to me entirely justified, and I set to work to bring a bit of variety to the evening, while still conserving its highly lyrical character. It was thus that I had the idea to add to the musical competition a little patriotic poem destined, in my mind, to rally all good French citizens..." What a pity that this contest never took place!

The Miserable Wretch and the Good Genie (*Le pauvre bougre et le bon génie*) was expanded into a one-act play in 1889, and published by Flammarion. It was first performed at the Théâtre des Mathurins on May 24, 1899. The miserable wretch and the waiter were played by Charles-Alexandre Guyon and a certain Réfy, respectively; the good genie was played by a Mademoiselle Dorville.

In 1903, the play was inserted into the ghost-written novel *Le Boomerang,* mentioned above in the notes to Silvérie.

In Scene 1, "O Matilda, idol of my soul" is from Rossini's *William Tell*; "Immortal glory of our ancestors" from Gounod's *Faust*; "What matter all these treacheries" from a song by Maurice Boukay.

A footnote in *The Boomerang* credits "Between the brunette and the blonde" (Scene 3) to Ferdinand Brunetière and the Abbé Cassine; that may not be true.

In Scene 5, "My children, I'm the anisette" is a parody of a song by Frédéric Bérat, concerning "La Lisette du chansonnier" ("The singer's Lisette").

Allais quoted the couplet that begins Scene 7 (in French, "C'est l'heure sainte / De l'absinthe") in his column in *Le Journal*, June 2, 1897. He added: "These two lines are by a poet who died young, and whom we were accustomed to baptize Maurice Donnay." La Belle Jardinière (The Beautiful Gardener) was Paris's first department store, opened in 1824.

In Scene 9, "When shall we be in cherry time" is a song by Jean Baptiste Clément and Antoine Renard.

The English Accent (*L'Accent anglais*) appeared in *Le Sourire*, December 9, 1899. In the fifth paragraph, the original reads "initiation servile," but I suspect a misprint, and have translated accordingly.

The Lycée Condorcet was founded in Paris in 1803; its alumni include Toulouse-Lautrec, Verlaine, Henri Bergson, Tristan Bernard, Sartre, and Proust.

The Polisher (*L'Astiqueur*) was written in 1900 with Albert-René Morice, and performed at the Théâtre du Gymnase on February 3, 1900. It appears to have been shelved after that. The reference to d'Ache is to the cartoonist Caran d'Ache, I suppose.

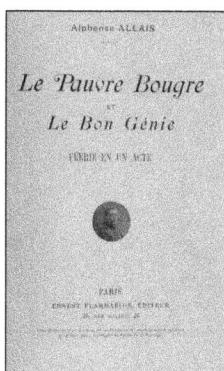

Appendix: Photographs from the Paris production of

Le Pauvre Bougre et Le Bon Génie

Alphonse ALLAIS

Le Pauvre Bougre

ET

Le Bon Génie

FÉERIE EN UN ACTE

PARIS

ERNEST FLAMMARION, ÉDITEUR

26, RUE RACINE, 26

Tous droits de reproduction, de traduction et de représentation réservés
pour tous pays, y compris la Suède et la Norvège.

Ô MATHILDE, IDOLE DE MON ÂME

GARÇON !

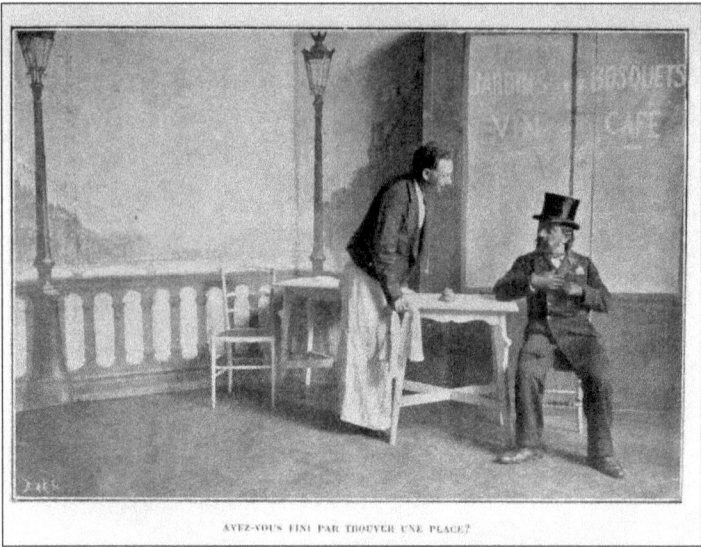

AVEZ-VOUS FINI PAR TROUVER UNE PLACE?

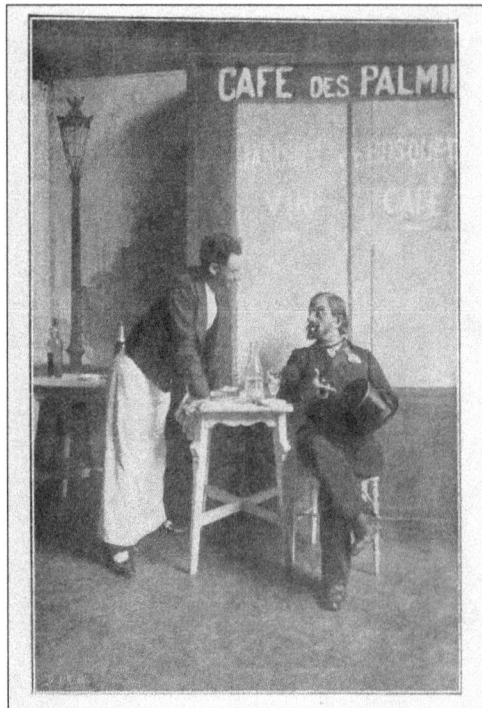

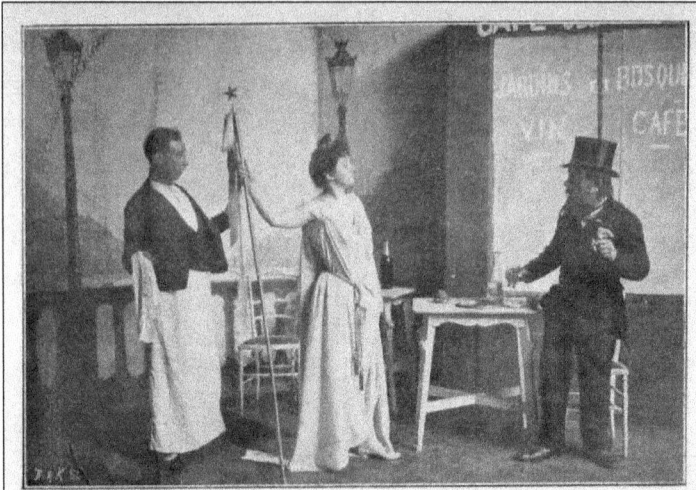

QUOI!... VOUS SERIEZ?...

JE NE FAIS QU'ALLER ET VENIR

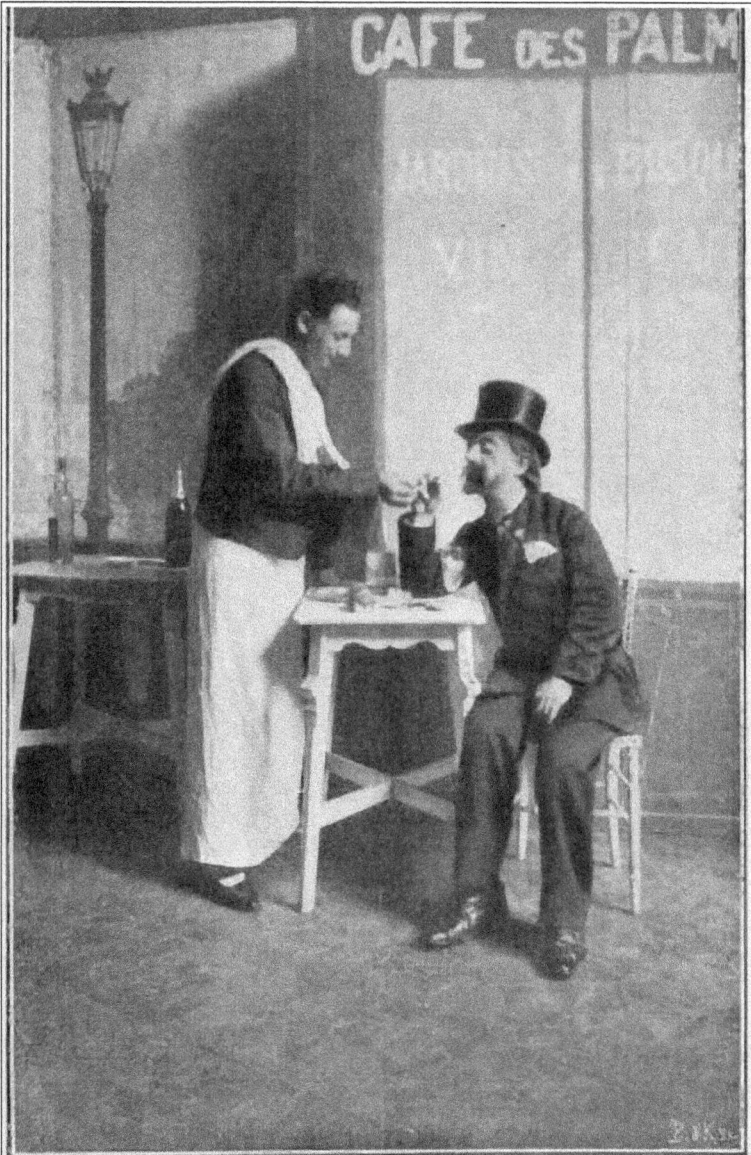

J'AI DROIT A CENT SOUS

REBONJOUR, PAUVRE BOUGRE!

PERNOD PUR, PERNOD BADIEUX!

ABOUT THE TRANSLATOR

Doug Skinner has written many scores for dance and theater, particularly for actor/clown Bill Irwin. He has contributed to *Fate, Fortean Times, Nickelodeon, Weirdo, Strange Attractor Journal, Black Scat Review,* and other periodicals. His translation of G. B. Nazari's *Three Dreams* was published in 2002 by Magnum Opus Hermetic Sourceworks in Glasgow. Black Scat Books has published several of his translations from the French, including Alphonse Allais's *Captain Cap: His Adventures, His Ideas, His Drinks* (2013), as well as a collection of his drawings, *The Unknown Adjective & Other Stories* (2014).